PR/ [partially covered by barcode sticker]

HOPE, HEALING, AND FREEDOM

"There has been a need for a practical and biblically-based guide for those struggling with pornography. *Hope, Healing, and Freedom* is that book. Although it is rooted in research, it also includes deeply personal insights and stories that will give you the hope and confidence that with grace, truth, community, and a proven strategy, porn addiction can be defeated."

SEAN MCDOWELL, PH.D., is a professor of Apologetics at Talbot School of Theology, the author of *Chasing Love: Sex, Love, and Relationships in a Confused Culture*, and a popular YouTuber

"This is a powerful, down-to-earth resource that will help you understand your struggle with porn and find God's redemption through it. Nick and Ashley don't just believe freedom from porn is possible, they have both personally experienced it. They bring biblical wisdom, personal stories, and scientific research to encourage you that you too can experience healing and freedom!"

DR. JULI SLATTERY, PH.D., president/co-founder of Authentic Intimacy, author of *Rethinking Sexuality* and *God, Sex, and Your Marriage*

"*Hope, Healing, and Freedom* is a powerful, compassionate guide for those navigating the pain of sexual struggles and betrayal trauma. Nick Stumbo and Ashley Jameson offer not only practical tools and hard-won insights, but a pathway to authentic transformation. This book is a gift to individuals, couples, and communities seeking healing and wholeness."

DR. JAKE PORTER, founder, Daring Ventures & International Association for Couple-Centered Recovery®

"*Hope, Healing, and Freedom* is a refreshingly honest and normalizing conversation about sexual compulsivity, betrayal trauma, and healing. With transparent personal stories and insight from decades of recovery ministry, Ashley and Nick offer readers compassionate support and a compass for transformation. This book is a treasure for individuals seeking healing and freedom. Every church needs this book!"

JENNA RIEMERSMA, LPC, CSAT-S, best-selling author of *Altogether You*

"All of us reach a point in our sexual lives when we quietly—or desperately—ask, *Is this it?* We long for, and were even promised, connection and beauty. But instead, we often find ourselves stuck in shame and disillusionment we can't seem to shake. Nick Stumbo and Ashley Jameson understand this terrain deeply. In *Hope, Healing, and Freedom*, they offer not only the heart of fellow travelers—those who know our pain and longings firsthand—but also the wisdom of seasoned guides who walk with us through the hardest valleys. Their remarkable kindness and knowledge invite us to consider that our sexual difficulties are not the end of the story, but an invitation to begin writing a more hopeful future."

JAY STRINGER, licensed mental health therapist and author of *Unwanted: How Sexual Brokenness Reveals Our Way to Healing* and *Desire: The Longings Inside Us and The New Science of How We Love, Heal, and Grow*

"Those who struggle personally with problematic sexual behavior, who have been betrayed by a struggler, or who want to help these individuals will all benefit from Pure Desire's *Hope, Healing, and Freedom.* Nick Stumbo and Ashley Jameson share vulnerably about their personal experiences with struggles, betrayal, and recovery, and they cut through the stereotypes about these issues. This much-needed book offers accurate information, practical strategies, and hope for a different future through a grace-filled Christian approach combined with sound clinical strategies."

MARNIE C. FERREE, MA, LMFT, CSAT, founder, Bethesda Workshops, author of *No Stones – Women Redeemed from Sexual Addiction* and *Out of the Doghouse for Christian Men*

"*Hope, Healing and Freedom* is a courageous and compassionate guide for anyone caught in the devastating cycle of sexual compulsivity or the life altering shock of betrayal. Written by two voices who know this journey intimately—this book offers not only deep insight, but a clear and redemptive path toward lasting recovery and restored relationships. What makes this book truly powerful is its authenticity. It does not shy away from the raw realities of pornography, sexual infidelity or the deep wounds it causes, yet it offers hope through Nick Stumbo and Ashley Jameson who as you will see are living billboards of real change."

DR. SHERI DENHAM KEFFER, author of *Intimate Deception: Healing the Wounds of Sexual Betrayal* and founder of The BraveOne Community

"We Christians tend to get a little squirrely when talking about pornography and compulsive sexual behavior. Sometimes we launch straight into Bible study, focusing on verses about lust. At other times we turn clinical, using only psychological and neurological terms. This book is different. In everyday language, Ashley Jameson and Nick Stumbo describe a proven program that is both biblically and scientifically sound. Their stories are relatable, their program reliable. This book is a must-read."

NATE LARKIN, founder of the Samson Society, author of *Samson and the Pirate Monks*

"How can the church become a place of healing for Christians struggling with unwanted sexual feelings? *Hope, Healing, and Freedom*, published by Pure Desire Ministries, offers compassionate and effective strategies. The authors introduce us to the findings of neuroscience, with its message that even deeply rooted behavioral patterns and compulsions can be changed. Neural pathways can be rewired. There is indeed hope and healing."

NANCY PEARCEY, professor and scholar in residence at Houston Christian University, and author of several bestselling books including *Total Truth* and *Love Thy Body*

"In a world drowning in sexual confusion and shame, Nick Stumbo and Ashley Jameson offer a Christ-centered path to hope, healing, and lasting freedom. As someone who's lived the devastation of sexual brokenness and now walks in restoration, I'm deeply grateful for resources like this—biblically faithful, clinically wise, and spiritually transformative."

JOSHUA BROOME, author, speaker, and Executive Director of Walk Worthy, AACC

"For anyone on the recovery journey from pornography, compulsive sexual behavior, and betrayal trauma, *Hope, Healing, and Freedom* is a must read. Through their honest and engaging experiences, Nick Stumbo and Ashley Jameson share their personal stories of struggle and redemption. With the right tools, a safe community, and the Holy Spirit active in your recovery, all things are possible!"

SHANNON ETHRIDGE, M.A., author of 22 books including *The Sexually Confident Wife*, *The Fantasy Fallacy*, and the million-copy best-selling *Every Woman's Battle* series

A PATHWAY BEYOND PORNOGRAPHY,
COMPULSIVE SEXUAL BEHAVIOR, AND BETRAYAL

HOPE HEALING AND FREEDOM

NICK STUMBO AND ASHLEY JAMESON

HOPE, HEALING, AND FREEDOM

Published by
Pure Desire Ministries International
www.puredesire.org | Troutdale, Oregon | August 2025
ISBN 978-1-943291-33-5

Content editing by Heather Kolb
Copy edited by Sue Miholer
Cover design, interior design, and typesetting by Elisabeth Windsor
Footprints from svstudioart on Freepik

CONTENTS

INTRODUCTION
IS THIS IT?

Have you ever found yourself in a place very different from where you expected to be? You thought you knew where you were going, what to expect, and what life would look like, and then one day you wake up only to realize you don't recognize anything. The world is not quite what you thought it would be. Your life didn't turn out how you thought it would.

In many ways, this is what our culture is experiencing in regard to the sexual landscape we find ourselves in, a place riddled with pornography, sexual dysfunction, and betrayal. Many set out with a particular view of sex, discover they have a distorted view, and are now wondering if this is as good as it gets—if this is really what sex and sexuality is all about.

Perhaps the biggest questions for anyone struggling with compulsive sexual behaviors are these:

- Am I destined to struggle with this forever?
- Is this my life?
- Is there any hope for healing and freedom?

When I (Nick) was a kid, I spent a great deal of my childhood traveling around the expansive states of Montana, Wyoming, and the Dakotas in the back seat of the family car. In that part of the world, a road trip is a serious commitment, a long-haul experience, and I remember mile after mile after mile, just staring out the window, watching the countryside go by. I was excited to get to our vacation destination, but sometimes getting there could be a bit tedious.

There wasn't much to break up the scenery, especially when we hit those long, seemingly never-ending plains, but I did start to notice a system of billboards that advertised for a specific destination. These billboards stood right along the highway, always reminding you precisely how far away you were from this incredible place. The prominence and size of the billboards, and the way they counted down the miles, aroused my curiosity. I was pretty sure this place must be a big deal.

The place the billboards advertised was known as Wall Drug in South Dakota. Because the states we traveled through were so large, and because they put up these signs all over, it wasn't unusual to see a billboard that said you still had 400 miles until Wall Drug. The other thing they always had on the signs, besides the miles remaining, was the offer of free ice water.

Wall Drug. 200 miles. Free ice water.

We went years and years without ever pulling off the exit and actually visiting Wall Drug, so in my mind the place grew to something of nearly mythic proportions. I wasn't even completely sure what I expected Wall Drug to be like, but surely all of those billboards pointed people to something rather incredible. I looked forward to the day my parents finally decided we were going to stop there on one of our road trips, imagining something akin to Disney World, or maybe a shopping mall of epic proportions.

Then came the day we stopped at Wall Drug.

When I was around 14 years of age and my family and I were on a trip through the Black Hills, my dad finally decided we were going to stop at Wall Drug. Oh, man, I couldn't believe it! After seeing all those billboards for all those years, I would finally get to experience this place of legend. I watched the miles on those billboards count down from 175 miles to 100 miles to 50 miles to 10 miles. Then, we arrived.

So what did I think about Wall Drug once I was finally able to see it in person?

Let me just put it this way: I had anticipated much, much more than what I found. Wall Drug was nothing more than a large rectangular building, a glorified drugstore. Inside, there were tourist items for sale, T-shirts, snacks, and drinks. And, true to their word, off in the corner was a little cooler of free ice water.

I remember just walking around the store in a bit of a daze, looking up and down the aisles, feeling more and more confused.

This is the place I've wanted to visit my entire childhood?

Is this it?

I (Ashley) have my own story of disappointment. We all do. Each of us is introduced to the concept of sex in unique ways, whether positive or negative, and these introductions go a long way in forming our sexual landscape when we get older. Like Nick's Wall Drug story, we all create an image of sex in our minds, and what a sexual relationship will be like, based on all sorts of different things. We can probably bet that Wall Drug would not have grown into this massive bucket list item for Nick if someone had told him it's simply a giant drugstore with cheap T-shirts. Having information helps us let go of the "need to know"—something that can get us into trouble when applied to compulsive sexual behaviors.

For me, my story brought me to the place where I was a divorced, single mom of twins, believing I would never remarry. I lived outside of a larger city, and worked as a supervisor in a doctor's office. My 4-year-old twin boys had already been through so much. I didn't want to risk dragging them through anything else or end up divorced again. I experienced extreme betrayals, but I had also made my own fair share of questionable choices in the past. I figured this was just how life was going to look for me.

Then everything changed. I met a great Christian guy who was okay with the fact that my past wasn't perfect because his wasn't either. We married when my twins were 5, and this time, I was determined to do things right and make godly choices. I would work harder this time. I thought I knew what I was getting into.

I left my job to move with my new husband to a small town, population of 700, but it felt worth it. We quickly had two more kids, and I became the stay-at-home mom I always dreamed of being. I was wrapped up again in the early stages of caring for babies and raising kids. Sometimes, it felt like I was drowning in diapers. I kept telling myself this marriage would be different. We were happy, everything was out in the open, and he was a Christian.

Then, four years into the marriage, secrets surfaced. My husband was using pornography and lying about it, making me feel crazy for asking. He also never disclosed that he had a past with prostitutes. He knew I had major trust issues from my previous relationships. I had a history of abuse and betrayal. I had decided I would never trust anyone again and would take care of myself and the twins. Yet, I laid this all to the side and married the first man I'd ever trusted—only to be lied to, manipulated, deceived, gaslit, and betrayed again. I felt all the wind rush out of my sails. I felt I had been tricked, brought to this small town only to be betrayed and stranded. Why would he marry me, move me away from all of my friends, and entangle my boys in this family story, only to have it lead to another failed marriage?

I was so angry, with God and with my husband. I tried to do things the right way. I took a risk. I let myself be vulnerable, and yet, here I was again. I felt abandoned by my new husband and God. The emotional and sexual aspects of our marriage fell apart. I was so crushed, scared for my future, and hopeless.

I didn't want to get another divorce and drag our four kids through that, but I didn't know what else to do. I had little hope that he could change or that I could ever feel the same way about him. It seemed the only choice was to leave him or to stay in a marriage devoid of trust and hope.

Maybe I just needed to learn to live with this pain—maybe this was simply part of it.

I thought this Christian marriage, and the sexual part of this relationship, would be different, better. But I found myself wondering, *Is this it? Will we never be free of this?*

For many of us, the sexual landscape of our own lives might feel the same, as we find ourselves in a place where our sexual experience is very different from what we expected (or hoped) it would be.

Maybe we're disappointed and ashamed, not because someone else has let us down, but because it's us—we're the one who has struggled, finding ourselves caught up in compulsive sexual behaviors we never thought we'd engage in, feeling imprisoned for longer than we thought possible, and experiencing results in our lives much more costly than we ever expected. We realize that somehow we've arrived at this point where the sexual element of our lives is primarily made up of shame, regret, and broken promises to ourselves and others.

We wish we could change it, but we haven't been able to.

Is this it? so many of us wonder. *Sex is nothing more than this thing that has taken over and ruined my life and the lives of those around me.*

Or maybe we find ourselves in this unexpected place because someone else—someone we love—is struggling through things we never imagined they would struggle with, and they've let us down in painful, heartbreaking ways. Maybe they've become disinterested in us because of their sexual struggles. We're now aware of what they've done, and sex feels like a place we're not sure we want to go anymore. Trust is broken.

Is this it? Sex is nothing more than emotional pain and disappointment and a reminder of how I've been betrayed and abused?

Maybe we're simply looking out at the sexual brokenness and pain in our world and are convinced this isn't what God intended. This isn't what God created the sexual experience to be. We have friends who have divorced because of compulsive sexual behaviors and other friends who we know are struggling with porn, and even family members who struggle. We know of kids who have been sexually abused or stumbled on to pornographic material, resulting in confusion, acting out, and distorted views of sex.

Is this it? Sex is nothing more than a negative force that's destroying the world around me?

A part of our lives we thought would be beautiful, joyful, and pleasurable has turned out to be a place of mistrust, brokenness, and shame. More and more people, having found themselves in an adulthood surrounded by sexual dysfunction seem to be wondering the same thing.

- How is this sexual dysfunction impacting our world?
- How is it changing the way people view sex and things like pornography, prostitution, and unfaithfulness?
- How does our sexually saturated culture contribute to the way men and women treat each other?
- Will any meaningful change happen? Is meaningful change even possible, or do these behaviors and struggles run too deep?

A recent Barna report states,

> *We're witnessing a generational pendulum swing regarding pornography: Once taboo and sparingly consumed during the heyday of Elders and Boomers, porn became accepted and normalized for Gen X and Millennials. However, Gen Z, having come of age in an era of unparalleled exposure, are gathering momentum for a pendulum swing back to a more critical stance. This shift may signify a broader cultural reassessment of pornography's role and impact, indicating a potential recalibration of societal attitudes toward explicit content.*[1]

Clearly, younger generations have witnessed firsthand the destruction caused by porn and other sexual addictions. Approximately, 50% of Gen Z responded that porn is either very bad or somewhat bad for our society, the highest percentage of any generation.[2]

Younger people have entered the sexual landscape of adulthood, a landscape in many ways formed by Gen X and Millennials, and they recognize the dysfunction, the unhealthiness, and the unsustainability.

---

[1] Pure Desire Ministries, *Beyond the Porn Phenomenon: Equipping the Church for a New Conversation about Pornography, Betrayal Trauma, and Healing* (Ventura: Barna Group, 2024), 31-32.

[2] Pure Desire Ministries, *Beyond the Porn Phenomenon*, 31.

They're starting to not only wonder, *Is this it?*

They're starting to seek out meaningful change.

But even if we want to change, where do we begin? We're left wondering what it takes to truly change. Those of us who struggle, and those of us who have tried to help someone who struggles, recognize that change in this area is not easy. Our brains are hardwired to avoid pain and seek pleasure, and few things are more pleasurable than sex.

So what do we do now? Like a child arriving at an underwhelming vacation stop, so many of us find ourselves here, in this place, wondering, *Is this it?*

- *Will I always struggle sexually?*
- *Will I ever be able to stop watching porn?*
- *Will my spouse quit or will they be like this for the rest of their life?*
- *Will my spouse ever understand how I've been hurt, and can I ever fully trust them again?*
- *Even if I can stop, will I spend the rest of my life "white-knuckling it," constantly having to dismiss temptation and fight against these desires to act out?*

You don't have to always struggle.

You can stop compulsive sexual behaviors.

Your loved one can change.

And this change we're talking about? It doesn't have to be the kind of change that feels like "white-knuckling it" for the rest of your life—you can experience a change that brings about peace, healing, and wholeness.

There is hope. You can find healing and freedom.

While those of us who are Christians have the incredible power of the Holy Spirit in our corner, sometimes being a Christian can add to the weight of what we're struggling with. This can happen because we know all the Bible verses that promise freedom, and yet many of us still can't experience that freedom.

"I can do all things through Christ who strengthens me."

PHILIPPIANS 4:13 (NKJV)

"Sin is no longer your master, for you no longer live under the requirements of the law. Instead, you live under the freedom of God's grace."

ROMANS 6:14 (NLT)

"And so I tell you, keep on asking, and you will receive what you ask for. Keep on seeking, and you will find. Keep on knocking, and the door will be opened to you. For everyone who asks, receives. Everyone who seeks, finds. And to everyone who knocks, the door will be opened."

LUKE 11:9–10 (NLT)

It's hard to know what to do when the Bible promises freedom and answered prayer when we're not experiencing it. It's hard to know what to think when Jesus promises healing and we're not seeing it. We've always been told that if we have enough faith in Jesus, all will work out—when it doesn't, we start to wonder what's wrong with us. Does this mean we've fallen too far away from God to ever feel His love again? Does this mean our past and present failures are simply too great to overcome, too big of a hurdle for us to get over?

If we can't make better choices, some of us start to feel that this disqualifies us from following Christ.

I (Ashley) remember people asking me if I was reading my Bible, praying, trusting, and forgiving, all while I was in pain I couldn't escape from. The trauma from betrayal wouldn't ease regardless of what spiritual thing I tried, and I began to wonder if I wasn't a good enough Christian. I wondered if there was something wrong with my faith because I couldn't simply "let go and let God."

When we don't overcome our compulsive sexual behaviors, we can begin to believe we're too weak, perhaps even unfit for the Kingdom of Heaven. But this isn't the case. For most of us who continue to struggle with compulsive sexual behaviors and addictions, the problem isn't that we're a bad Christian or that Jesus doesn't love us anymore.

The real problem is that we're trying to set out on this journey ill-equipped and alone.

There's another life waiting for all of us beyond sexual struggles and acting out, beyond betrayal and abuse—not a life of constantly failing, not even a life where we struggle day after day to resist our old ways of acting out. And for most of us, it's not about simply trying harder or even memorizing another Bible verse.

Our goal with this book is to show you a comprehensive path to healing, wholeness, and freedom, a path that addresses not only the spiritual element (which is essential), but also the biological and relational sides to the issue. It's a journey that thousands of people have been introduced to and one that has led them into a healthy and whole way of experiencing what sex can really be about.

As we embark on this journey together, you'll begin to recognize how your compulsive sexual behaviors are actually a pseudo-solution to very real and legitimate needs. We'll explore how God's design for sex lines up with our innate physiological desires and needs. God created our sexuality. Our sexuality is good.

Our view toward sex doesn't have to be, *Is this it?*

There is true freedom to be found.

Sex can be restored as a thing of beauty and connection in our lives—an area that brings joy, fulfillment, and pleasure without the guilt, shame, and regret.

That's what this book is all about.

PART ONE

WHERE WE ARE

CHAPTER ONE
THE WIDE PATH

Where do we begin when talking about our current culture's relationship with sex?

Too many people struggle silently with compulsive sexual behaviors, the kind that are ruining their lives—relationally, spiritually, financially. But because most people keep this area of their lives a secret, it can be difficult to understand the true scope of the situation.

Perhaps we start by acknowledging the numbers.

As of 2024, nearly four in five men (78%), and nearly half of all women, admit to using pornography.[3]

About two in five Gen Z and Millennials take in pornographic content daily or weekly.

The 2024 study also has shown there is little difference in the daily and weekly porn habits between Christians and non-Christians.

We don't set out to become addicted or to have an affair or to ruin relationships with people we love—these aren't life goals for most people. Often, these behaviors spin out of control,

---

[3] Pure Desire Ministries, *Beyond the Porn Phenomenon*, 22.

and while we don't often see the day-to-day behavior, we do occasionally bear witness to the disastrous results. So why do so many of us find ourselves dabbling in, and then struggling with, things that have the potential to ruin our lives?

For me (Nick), my first real exposure to graphic nudity was at a friend's house, where we watched an NC-17-rated slasher film that had tons of gratuitous nudity. When the first naked woman appeared on screen, my adolescent mind locked in: *What am I seeing? My parents would be angry if they knew what I was watching. This feels wrong. But I'm also very intrigued. I like it, and I want to see more, but I'm already feeling ashamed.*

There's a push-pull in our early exposure to sexuality. Because I wasn't having conversations about this with my parents, and because it felt embarrassing and shameful, I assumed that the part of me that was intrigued was sinful. As I got older, that feeling was reinforced by a continued silence around the topic—something's wrong with me, I shouldn't be interested in these things, sexuality is shameful and wrong.

This is a common starting point for so many people, and the push-pull, the shameful feelings, become even more intense when our initial sexual encounters involve abuse or rape. Whether our first exposure to nudity or something much worse, the message that settles into our brain is the same: there's a part of me that's drawn to it, so my sexuality must be sinful and bad. We begin to associate our pleasure, which is God-ordained, with sinfulness.

The challenge for us as we get older is that the association doesn't disappear—somehow our pleasure remains sinful in our minds. In church we only ever hear that sex is for marriage and we're impure if we do anything sexual outside of that.

But God created us as sexual beings. Pleasure in sexuality is God's gift to us, and we'll talk more about that later in the book.

As we move into and through recovery work, it can suddenly become clear: the root of many sexual addictions and compulsive sexual behaviors began in our childhood, when we were exploring and didn't know what to do with all of these new feelings and experiences.

These stories aren't unusual. It's quite common for circumstances from our childhood or our teenage years to lead us unexpectedly into a version of sexuality we never would have chosen. Some kids are introduced to pornography at an early age. For some, curiosity leads to the pattern, and pattern leads to compulsion. Addictive behavior can become a coping mechanism for loss or pain or disappointment. Sometimes it's easy to believe that everyone else is doing it, too, right? So we start exploring, then find ourselves caught in a pattern of destructive, addictive behaviors that spiral further and further out of control.

Typically, we hear a common response.

Addiction?

I'm not addicted to these behaviors.

It's not that serious.

Early on in my (Nick) journey to recovery, my wife and I had heard about Pure Desire at an event for pastors in our denomination, but to be honest, I didn't want to go. I didn't think my problem was that serious, and I certainly didn't think I needed that kind of intense help, but my wife knew we did. She could recognize it for what it was.

So, since she thought we should explore it a little more, I went to meet with a coach in our denomination who would help me determine if Pure Desire was the right next step. This coach was a friend of mine, and I proceeded to spend about an hour explaining to him my current situation in regard to pornography and why it wasn't that big of a deal. Besides, the program Pure Desire had was too long, too expensive, and would be too invasive for my life. I wanted a quick fix, and I truly believed I only needed a little bit of help to get back on track.

"I'm doing pretty good now," I insisted. "I just need some minor fixes, and then I'll be good as new. I'm very close."

"Okay, Nick," he replied. "I hear you. Let me ask you a few questions. First, how long has this been a problem?"

"Well," I admitted. "You know as well as anyone that it's been a long road. I was first exposed to porn as a kid, then stole a *Playboy* when I was 15. So, it's been around 15 years or so that this has been a problem for me."

"Okay, second question. How many times have you tried to stop?"

I actually laughed a bit at this one. "Every time I did it, that was the last time. Never again. That's what I always say—God,

I promise you I'm done." I paused. "I guess if that's true, I've tried to stop hundreds of times."

He nodded his head. "Third question: is it causing you or the people you love significant pain?"

At this point I could see where we were going. I sighed. "Yes. I think if I don't change, my wife is going to leave, because she's so hurt by it."

He heard me out, waited a moment, and then went on. "Let's put those three things together. It's been a problem for a long time, and you've tried to change without success, even though it's causing significant pain in your life."

"Yeah, that's a pretty good summary of my life right there."

"Nick, that's the clinical definition of an addiction. It's been a problem for a long time and you've been unable to change in spite of the consequences that are happening in your life."

I sat back in my chair and felt like he had just punched me. I didn't think a pastor like me could be an addict—to me, an addict was an identity, an addict was personified by people who were addicted to drugs or who went out and paid for prostitutes. I "just" looked at porn every once in a while. I had never thought about what I was doing as an addiction.

Seventy-seven percent of porn users believe a person can both regularly view porn and live a sexually healthy life, while 59% of the same porn users believe porn addiction is not a real condition or a legitimate concern.[4] You can see the disconnect here: people

---

[4] Pure Desire Ministries, *Beyond the Porn Phenomenon*, 72.

believe addiction to porn is possible and even dangerous … we just don't think it's us.

It's important to say here that labeling something as an addiction doesn't remove our responsibility for our actions. I had made every decision that led me to this place. Calling this state addiction simply helps us understand the severity of the place we're in and hopefully recognize the kind of help we really need.

But it was helpful for me to see my behavior as an addiction—it explained why, in all of my sincerity to change, I wasn't changing. In all my efforts to stop, I wasn't stopping. There was more going on in my brain, more happening in my way of believing and thinking, and more going on in my way of managing life that combined and meant I couldn't simply try harder in order to stop.

I had tried harder for 15 years. It hadn't worked.

I needed a new framework.

I finally recognized the severity of what was happening.

Unfortunately, these unintentionally developed addictions, these coping mechanisms, often do lead to destruction. But what kind of destruction? How serious is it, really?

For one, according to data from the General Social Survey, "people who started watching porn were more likely to split with their partners during the course of the survey. For men, the chance of divorce went from 5% to 10%. For women, that number jumped from 6% to 18%."[5]

Another study found that within couples in an intimate relationship, porn can cause the following challenges:[6]

- Users face difficulty becoming sexually aroused without pornography.
- Users lose interest and engage in fewer sexual experiences with their partner.
- Pornography consumption may be correlated with increased behaviors of hooking up and infidelity.
- Partner feels sexually inadequate and threatened by pornography use.
- Partners may feel that certain sexual activities desired by users are objectionable.
- Both user and partner experience decreased relationship sexual satisfaction and emotional closeness.
- Relationship trust decreases due to dishonesty and deception about pornography use.
- Both user and partner experience lower relationship satisfaction and stability, less positive communication, and more psychological aggression between partners.

---

[5] David Shultz, "Divorce rates double when people start watching porn," *Science*, August 26, 2016, https://www.science.org/content/article/divorce-rates-double-when-people-start-watching-porn.

[6] Naomi Brower, "Effects of Pornography on Relationships," Utah State University, April 2023, https://extension.usu.edu/relationships/research/effects-of-pornography-on-relationships.

The stats seem overwhelming, and the pattern of destruction well-documented, but who's actually involved in this kind of stuff?

Maybe you have an image in your mind of the kinds of people who typically struggle with these addictive behaviors. Maybe you think of sleazy men cat-calling women on the street, or women who talk or act a certain way. Maybe when you think of sexual addiction, you think of the lonely old man locked up in his apartment, or the awkward teenager who spends all hours online.

The truth is, those who struggle with sexual addiction look a lot like me and a lot like you.

Here are just three of the stories we've heard over the years. While these are individual stories, they share common traits with many of those who have spoken with us.

Kurt was a typical kid, growing up in a nice, Christian home. His family went to church every Sunday. They read the nativity story in the Bible before opening their presents on Christmas morning. He studied hard at school and tried not to lie, cheat, or steal. And his family certainly never talked about anything sexual—books and movies that had anything in them having to do with sex were off-limits, so there didn't seem to be much of a reason to bring it up.

Sexual meant sinful, at least in Kurt's childhood eyes. And no one wanted to talk about it.

You can imagine 8-year-old Kurt's surprise, while playing with his teenage cousin in his room, when his cousin showed him a

Playboy magazine. All those naked women. So many things Kurt didn't understand … and was intrigued by. He didn't want to keep looking, and he didn't want to look away. To be honest, the whole situation scared him … and brought about an incredible curiosity, like nothing he had experienced before.

Not too much later, he discovered a stash of similar magazines in his father's workbench in the garage, and that was enough to keep him going back. Even though he had this feeling in his gut that what he was doing was wrong, that he was being dishonest, that these weren't things he should be looking at, he returned to the magazines in the workbench over and over again. It became a big part of his young life.

Pornography.

When he got his first computer as a teenager, it didn't take long for him to realize he could access free porn, and that's when it became a weekly habit, then almost daily. Looking at porn—when he was bored, when he was up late at night, when he was discouraged about something—became just a normal part of his life. And because his parents didn't even have a clue that these kinds of things were available online, he barely had to hide it.

It wasn't until he got married that he considered giving up porn. The sense that what he was doing was wrong had never completely gone away. But maybe he wouldn't have to confess it or get any kind of special help—maybe having regular, "godly" sex would cure him of his desire to look at porn. Maybe this thing he couldn't quite shake free from would fade away once he had a wife, this habit becoming something he would someday remember and shake his head at. Something buried in the past.

Maybe getting away from it would be easy, something he could do on his own.

But despite being in a good marriage, he kept going back to porn. He would tell himself this was the last time; he wanted to quit; his wife would be so upset if she found out … but four to six weeks later he'd be back. It always left him feeling disengaged from his wife, like there was something between them. He lashed out at her in anger, even though he knew he was only angry and frustrated with himself and his inability to make the change he wanted to make.

Life went on. He stayed in church, though the guilt was sometimes overwhelming. Eventually he was asked to serve on the deacon board of his church, something that made his porn addiction feel even worse! Now he was a leader, someone everyone else looked up to. The hypocrisy made him feel sick.

He didn't think he could ever tell anyone at church about this issue; in fact, now that he was in leadership, he became more determined to hide it than ever before. Sometimes, at the board meetings, he'd look around the table and think he must be the only one struggling with a porn addiction. Surely the other members of the church's leadership team didn't have the same problem. When he was asked to pray to close the meeting, he harbored such deep shame that he almost couldn't do it. And when he was finally able to pray, he thought to himself that there was no way God listened to his prayers. Not after all these years of acting out and sinful behavior.

Soon after that, he decided to give it up for good. For real. This time. He would be serious. This was it.

But he couldn't quit. Four weeks later, his wife was out with some friends and he was right back on his phone, looking at images that had haunted him since he was 8.

After so many years of trying to stop on his own, he has given up hope of ever changing—he figures this is just his "cross to bear," and that someday, hopefully, he'll come to understand why he can't overcome this addiction.

In the meantime, life goes on and he feels more and more shame. But he can't quit.

When Keisha was 9, her mom started taking her along to R-rated movies—they couldn't afford a babysitter, and, besides, Keisha's mom covered her eyes during the sex scenes. But Keisha often wondered what was going on in those scenes her mother hid from her, so when she got older she started replaying those R-rated scenes on TV at home and masturbating when her mom was at work or sleeping.

She felt bad about what she was doing, but for some reason it was something she couldn't stop.

When Keisha was a teenager, she got a phone with social media, and she discovered she could watch sexually arousing content privately without worrying about someone else finding out—she began looking forward to bedtime, when she could retreat to her room, watch whatever she wanted, and masturbate.

When she moved out of the house, masturbation became almost a necessity to get through the day. But social media wasn't arousing any longer, so she started searching for porn. Her shame levels went through the roof—she was a Christian, knew looking at porn was wrong, and understood that it contributed to sex trafficking and the mistreatment of women and girls. On one hand, she wondered why she couldn't quit … but she always said one more time. One more time, and then she'd be finished with it.

And so it continued.

Keisha tried attending more Bible studies, praying daily for God to take the urge away, and she even went so far as getting rid of her only TV, but when none of that worked, she felt hopeless and disappointed in God because He wouldn't help her. She withdrew from her friends at church because she felt like a fraud.

She started attending more parties with her friends outside of church, which led to drinking and one-night stands with strangers. After one particularly scary sexual incident, she vowed off partying.

That lasted for a few weeks, until her friends eventually talked her into going out again, and the same things started right back up.

Keisha wondered if God could still love her after all the things she'd done. She doubted it.

She wondered if getting married might help her to stop acting out sexually.

She wondered if there was any way to change this life she was living.

Bill did two things when he was 18 that not many of his friends had done: he joined the Marine Corps and he got engaged. He was completely in love with his high school sweetheart, and they decided they'd get married after he returned from his first deployment. He was excited to get out and see the world, and joining the Corps helped give him a sense of purpose and belonging. He loved it, and he carried a photo of his fiancée with him everywhere. Life seemed to be just about as good as it could get.

But on his first deployment, he realized that if he was going to fit in, he was going to have to do some things he wasn't comfortable with. Some of these things involved physical training and persevering through exercises and situations where he would have normally quit. There were long days and sleepless nights, uniform inspections, and hellish marches through swamps and forests and up mountainsides. But the camaraderie of the Corps helped him get through, and he formed tight bonds with the guys in his unit.

The peer pressure wasn't always positive, though—the group sometimes pressured each other into doing things Bill didn't feel good about. One of those things was paying for sex with prostitutes, something that was common among his fellow Corps members, something they all joked about, and something that Bill ended up doing, too.

The first time he did it, he shrugged it off by saying he wasn't married yet, it wasn't a big deal, no one was hurt, the woman needed the money, his fiancée would never find out ... the excuses went on and on. But deep inside, he knew it wasn't right, and the experience left a kind of dark void in him—one he couldn't get rid of. He swore he'd stop after he got married.

Their wedding took place while he was home between deployments, and it was a beautiful day, one he'd never forget. But the entire day, he kept thinking of his experience overseas, hiring a prostitute, and wondering how he could make it right. He felt ashamed all day, especially when he saw how happy his bride was.

Six months later when he was back on deployment, as soon as he was out on a free night with his buddies, he did it again—hired a prostitute. He wasn't even sure why, other than it just seemed like something to do when he was away, and he justified it using the same old excuses.

- No one would find out.
- The woman needed the money.
- He was away for six months.

It would happen multiple times in the first five years of his marriage.

Early on, his wife suspected something, if only because it was clear that this kind of behavior was common in the Corps. She heard the stories. Her friends were the wives of other men in the Corps. But every time she pressed him for the truth, asking if he ever did these things the other men did, he insisted he had always been faithful. Eventually she stopped asking.

Thirty years later, Bill lives with this secret every day of his life. When he's with his kids and grandkids, he feels like a failure. Now that he and his wife are empty nesters, he looks at her and wonders what their life would have been like if he never would have done it. Would their marriage have been better, their connection stronger? When he goes to church, he believes he has disqualified himself from God's grace because of the sin he committed and his unwillingness to confess it.

Decades have passed. Decades have been tainted. Even though no one but Bill knows about it, this choice he made has had a real impact on his relationships with others. Not only that, but he has been pretty much shut down sexually most of his life, even with his wife. It's been an area of their marriage that has always felt like a struggle, but he doesn't want to address it because of the shame he feels regarding his past. He knows his wife would be devastated. He feels like he could never do that to her.

Not only does he avoid sex with his wife—he even avoids simply developing friendships with other men, because he's scared of what any kind of in-depth relationship might stir up. What if someone asks him about his past? What if they ask him about his time in the Marine Corps? What if they confess to lust or having a porn addiction and then ask him if he's ever struggled in the same way?

He believes that any exposure of his past would destroy everything, that his wife would never be able to forgive him, and that their relationship would crumble.

His church occasionally mentions the topics of lust and porn, but he's convinced his past sin goes way beyond anything that anyone at his church knows how to deal with, so he stays alone in his shame.

Bill isn't sure what to do.

These are only three of the many stories we have heard at Pure Desire, stories of men and women whose struggle with sexual addiction has ruined some aspect of their lives, damaged relationships, and riddled them with shame and self-doubt, some for nearly their entire lives. And while these are three individual stories, they are also representative of the thousands of people we've crossed paths with whose lives have been twisted under these same struggles.

Pornography.

Prostitution.

Affairs.

Hook-up culture.

These are the sexual struggles that are, unfortunately, beginning to define an entire culture and generation.

And yet there is hope! We help men and women every day! We see people come out of these addictions, their relationships restored, their inner lives healed.

There is a journey to healing and freedom.

CHAPTER TWO
THE STRUGGLER'S PROFILE

Before we set out on that journey though, it's important to wrestle with these questions:

What are the traits of a typical struggler? If we home in on those, can we then map out a path to healing?

Perhaps when you think of the stereotypical person with a sexual addiction, you think of the mugshots in the newspaper of men caught with illegal, underage porn in their possession, and the way they stare with empty eyes into the camera. Maybe you think of friends or loved ones who have had multiple affairs, whose lives have been ruined by their unfaithfulness. Or perhaps when you think of someone with a sexual addiction, you think of men and women arrested for prostitution, looking ashamed or upset.

Maybe the words "pervert" or "deviant" come to mind.

It's easy to see photos like that and think to ourselves,

- *That is one messed-up person.*
- *No one I know could ever have a sex addiction like that.*
- *I certainly never would!*

But what we've found through the years at Pure Desire is that the profile of those who struggle runs the entire spectrum of our society, from pastors to teachers, from ex-convicts to military heroes. From teenagers to the elderly. Men and women, young and old. No one is exempt from getting caught in the web of sexual addiction.

This isn't to say strugglers don't share anything in common, because they do. Here are just a few:

The struggler is isolated. If there's anything we've noticed through the years, it's the isolation of those who struggle—either an isolation from other people, or an isolation from anyone who can help them. They often feel this isolation in profound ways, and the shame and guilt surrounding their sexual addiction only serves to exacerbate their loneliness. This becomes a downward spiral—watching porn or acting out sexually leads to shame and guilt, which leads to them retreating from those around them, which leads to more isolation, then ultimately leads to watching more pornography or seeking comfort in their sexual addiction.

Those who struggle with pornography were asked who's helping them, with potential answers being their spouse, their pastor, a friend, a small group, or a counselor. Overwhelmingly, 82% replied that no one is helping them.[7] They are isolated in their struggle.

Who can we even go to in such a time, when so much shame and embarrassment is involved?

---

[7] Pure Desire Ministries, *Beyond the Porn Phenomenon: Equipping the Church for a New Conversation about Pornography, Betrayal Trauma, and Healing* (Ventura: Barna Group, 2024), 6.

People have responded that the number one person they would go to is a counselor, which makes sense and can be very helpful in discovering the root of the issue. (Going to a pastor was one of the last options people listed!)[8] Counselors can give people tools that will help them journey out of addiction. And yet even going to a counselor can be very isolating, because the visits are private and they're paid to listen and help. So when the struggler returns to their normal life, they still feel isolated, even as they're getting help.

The struggler is alone in their secrecy. This isolation leads to another commonality among strugglers: they don't tell anyone about their sexual habits. Their porn use isn't something they joke about or bring up with friends. If there is an affair, it's kept secret from those they love. And, in general, they're not pursuing relationships (friendships or counseling) where they can receive support from anyone else. They think those closest to them would reject them or be irreparably disappointed if they shared their struggles, so they remain silent.

Approximately, 51% of adults said no one even knows about their struggle.[9] But what about Christians? Surely those who are constantly taking in sermons and messages that emphasize confession and honesty are more forthright with their sexual struggles? But Christians said the same thing, with 49% responding that no one knows about their struggle with pornography.

This can be especially true of those in ministry—if they admit to their struggles, they could lose their job, their livelihood, and even their family. So they just keep going along, not sure where to go for help.

---

[8] Pure Desire Ministries, *Beyond the Porn Phenomenon*, 45.

[9] Pure Desire Ministries, *Beyond the Porn Phenomenon*, 13.

This loneliness isn't only felt by the person struggling—it can also be felt by the spouse of the struggling person if a confession is made, because they're not sure what steps to take or who to tell. The partner of a struggling person often feels there must be something wrong with them if their spouse needed to look outside the marriage for sexual satisfaction. They worry about the struggler losing their job and how it will impact their lifestyle, ministry, or parenting. They're ashamed and embarrassed for many different reasons, and sometimes the confession of their spouse can even lead to further isolation.

The struggler is sincere in their faith but stuck in a binge-purge cycle. The reality is that the rate of struggle and addiction among Christians is not that much different than the rates among non-Christians. Many people assume that if someone is struggling, they must not be that sincere in their faith. Maybe they're just calling themselves a Christian but don't have a real commitment to Jesus.

The fact is, this simply isn't true.

Many Christian strugglers still have a sincere faith, even while trying to navigate their sexual addiction. Often, they are praying repeatedly for God to take away this behavior. Many have had pastors tell them that their faith will heal them, only to go on and find it impossible to quit. Many go to confession and yet still continue struggling. Many times it's this sincerity that continually brings them to the point of making promises to themselves.

"I'll never do it again."

"This is the last time."

Often, after particularly intense binges on porn or unhealthy sexual activity, we try to purge our life of the addiction, canceling subscriptions to online porn websites, deleting apps, or breaking it off with friends who have enabled these behaviors.

But this binge-purge cycle is rarely, if ever, effective in bringing about lasting change.

The struggler believes it's wrong but also minimizes it. Barna's 2024 study into pornography use and sexual behaviors revealed some fascinating data surrounding the number of people who believe porn is wrong but who still engage in it. Forty-five percent of practicing Christians believe porn is "very bad" for society—even a quarter of non-Christians believe porn is very bad.[10] But when Christian adults in the U.S. with a personal history of porn use are asked how they feel about their own use of porn, 50% are comfortable with how much porn they use. Only 20% of Christians with a personal history of porn wish they didn't use it at all.[11]

Christians understand that it's wrong—we know that lust is sinful, and there are plenty of passages in Scripture about ridding ourselves of lustful thoughts and sexual immorality (Matthew 5:28, Colossians 3:5). And we believe that.

But there are also conflicting messages in the culture, and even among Christians, that allows the struggler to tell themselves it's not really that bad. "Boys will be boys," is a phrase that's thrown around in regard to watching porn (interestingly, it's never "Men

---

[10] Pure Desire Ministries, *Beyond the Porn Phenomenon*, 42.

[11] Pure Desire Ministries, *Beyond the Porn Phenomenon*, 35.

will be men"). And then there's the sense that since everyone is struggling with this, or nearly everyone, maybe I don't have to do anything about my own struggle.

- *I can't really help it.*
- *I was just created this way.*
- *I would never be able to change even if I tried.*

It can be very defeating when the message the struggler is hearing, often even at church, is that you should do your best but this is something you'll struggle with until the day you die. They wonder if they'll ever be able to walk in freedom, or if they're looking at a lifetime of sin management.

The struggler believes sexual addiction is real but doesn't think that label fits them. Often we think of addiction in terms of the scope or perceived severity of the behavior. We might think of watching porn in our own home as not being that destructive, not that serious. We can easily minimize our own addiction when we see other people paying for sex with prostitutes or watching hardcore porn all day. Approximately, 1 in 3 porn users (32%) agree with the statement, "Porn addiction is not a real condition or legitimate concern."[12]

But we need to begin to recognize that addiction is not about severity as much as it is about dependence.

Start by asking yourself the same questions Nick's spiritual coach asked him back in Chapter One:

- How long has it been a problem?

[12] Pure Desire Ministries, *Beyond the Porn Phenomenon*, 72.

- How many times have you tried to stop?
- Is it causing you or people you love significant pain?

For many of us, watching porn, even once a month, is something we've struggled with for a while, tried to stop, and is causing some level of pain in our lives or the lives of those we love. This might not seem that serious, but what's going on in our lives during the intervening days and weeks?

Some of us go to social media to look for triggering images, or we're going to the gym every day and checking out all the women or we're overeating—most of us wouldn't think of this as a serious problem. Did we even do anything wrong? But this can very much be part of our addictive cycle, so that it builds to the point where we have one night where we go too far on the internet, a line gets crossed, and we feel shame and regret.

The nature of addiction is that it creates an entire cycle of behavior.

Sexual addiction is not about sex. It's just one piece of the puzzle, one way we attempt to meet our needs in a way that's not helpful to us or those we're in relationship with.

The struggler is often harming their marriage, whether their spouse knows or not. There are so many negative things that happen within a relationship when one of the partners is looking at porn, even if the other person doesn't know about it.

First of all, because there's hiding, there's a constant level of dishonesty and gaslighting that takes place. One spouse might ask their struggling spouse, "Are you okay? What's wrong?" and because the struggler doesn't want their spouse to know, they deflect and lie. "Nothing's wrong! I just had a hard day at work," or, "The kids are really stressing me out." And because the struggling spouse isn't being honest, a disconnect begins. The betrayed spouse is left questioning their intuition and instinct. The struggler is not being transparent, something relationships are built on.

Second, science has shown that we bond to whatever it is that we are looking at or imagining when we orgasm.[13] Whenever someone reaches climax, the brain releases chemicals that cause a desire to bond. When someone is struggling with porn, they could be doing this multiple times a week or even multiple times a day, continually reinforcing this bond with someone/something other than their spouse, weakening their relationship in immeasurable ways.

Whenever someone comes to us and says they don't have the sex life they want, the first question we usually ask is, "Are you looking at porn?" So many times, the answer is yes, because watching porn always has a negative long-term impact on things like libido and emotional connection.

Finally, sex addictions lead to a numbing of emotions. God designed our brains to protect us from pain and help us pursue pleasure—we were created this way. So, if we have a secret that we know could potentially hurt our spouse, we try to avoid that pain and replace it with pleasure. Some turn to masturbation, porn, or other ways of acting out sexually, and that allows our brain to turn down the dial on the pain we're feeling.

---

[13] Blumenthal SA, Young LJ. "The Neurobiology of Love and Pair Bonding from Human and Animal Perspectives." *Biology (Basel)*. 2023;12(6):844. Published 2023 Jun 12. doi:10.3390/biology12060844.

But when we do this on a consistent basis, our ability to feel all emotions is turned down. We have spouses of strugglers come to us and say their partners are emotionally disengaged—this is because of the secrecy and pain avoidance. Often, when people pursue healing, their emotions return. They'll say things like, "Wow! I can cry again!" or, "I forgot how it felt to experience delight and play." They didn't realize how much they had to numb their senses in order to live in that secrecy, and it was impacting their marriage at a very emotional level.

The struggler is any age, gender, or at any level of spiritual maturity. Many people think about their acting out with porn or even paying for sex and think, *Eventually, I'll mature and grow out of this. Someday, I'll just stop.*

This couldn't be further from the truth. In fact, the longer we let these things exist in our lives, the harder it will be to walk away. If it's an issue in our teens and twenties and we don't deal with it, it will follow us into our thirties, forties, fifties, and sixties. We've had people come through the Pure Desire program anywhere from their late teens through their eighties!

Once, we even had two of those guys in the same group, at the opposite end of the age spectrum. They were listening to the same lies, had the same challenges, even though the 19-year-old was battling videos on his smartphone while the 81-year-old was driving an hour to the adult bookstore to pick up videos that he'd take home and watch.

Their methods were very different, but what drove them was very similar: a need to feel loved, seen, and valued.

It's so easy to look at some people and think they seem so well-adjusted, have a healthy marriage, seem to have a good family and great kids, and have a well-paying job, so there's no way he or she is struggling with porn. But you really can't judge a book by its cover—someone who looks like that on the outside may be a wreck internally. Sex addiction can be so hidden and embedded in someone's life that you'd never guess they struggle with it.

The struggler wants to be free but doesn't know what it might take. In our experience, the overwhelming majority of strugglers want to be free but cannot see a path forward. While there are certainly those who begin coming to a group because their spouse caught them and said they have to change or the relationship is over, even that can often lead to a genuine desire to quit—they want to save their relationship.

Most want to be free. Most want this burden out of their life. But when we feel immense shame and hopelessness, we can stop trying and give up.

Often, it takes a relationship crisis or the awareness of how we're hurting someone in order to really push us into making that change. As Tony Robbins has said, "Change happens when the pain of staying the same is greater than the pain of change."[14]

The other part of this is that many of us are afraid we can never be truly free of our sex addiction. We think that what waits for us in sobriety is a kind of white-knuckling experience, a life where we're constantly struggling to say no to porn or whatever other sexual acting out has ruled our lives. It can be overwhelming,

[14] Tony Robbins, *11 Powerful Health Quotes*, **https://www.tonyrobbins.com/tony-robbins-quotes/health-quotes**.

believing that we're going to be miserable the rest of our life, fighting these urges.

But the truth is, freedom is possible. It might be difficult in the beginning and feel like there's very little hope, but the majority of us who commit to the process at Pure Desire experience true healing, a renewing of our mind in which our desires actually change.

The struggler questions the love of God and even their own faith. When Christians can't recover from an addiction on their own, typically the church encourages them to try harder. Have more faith. Read your Bible more often. Pray more. Confess again. A favorite verse brought up within the church when it comes to addiction is John 8:34–36:

> *Jesus replied, "Very truly I tell you, everyone who sins is a slave to sin. Now a slave has no permanent place in the family, but a son belongs to it forever. So if the Son sets you free, you will be free indeed."*

This sounds great right? If the Son sets you free, you'll be free indeed.

If you're a "slave to sin," you have no permanent place in God's family.

That's harsh, but those are Jesus' words, right?

But what happens when Christians keep struggling? Many have verses like these thrown in their face and walk away feeling like they must not be true followers of Christ if they can't kick whatever habit it is they're struggling with. Struggling Christians simply keep "trying harder," but when they don't make progress, the shame cycle deepens.

They pray even harder, get an accountability partner, or go to counseling. All good things, but what if they still can't find freedom?

At Pure Desire, we believe the power of Jesus is here to set people free. We believe God can miraculously heal people. But many people in our groups have tried these things—prayer, confession, memorizing Bible verses—and then on the way home, or perhaps the next day, they find themselves right back where they started. They wonder if God loves them, or if they're even true believers.

While all of those things about Jesus are true—He is here to set people free from sin—and while all of those practices are beneficial, often, somewhere along the way, shame, trauma, and other difficult life experiences keep that message of love from moving from our heads to our hearts. We need help unpacking our stories so we can pinpoint where these deceitful messages about Christ and about ourselves took root.

The betrayal felt by partners of those who struggle is real. People mistakenly refer to porn use as a "victimless crime." Because there's no physical contact between the viewer and those being viewed, and because the act is most often done in isolation, how can anyone else be harmed? How can there be any real-world impact?

Pornography is not a victimless crime. There is the exploitation and trafficking of those in the industry, especially women and young girls. And there is the betrayal felt by the partners of those who become dependent on porn.

Many people believe that if the spouse didn't actually have a physical affair with someone else, the betrayed spouse can't experience any true trauma, but this simply is not the case. Betrayal trauma is real, and most partners who discover that their spouse has been using porn experience this trauma.

In *Beyond the Porn Phenomenon*, the research found that "damaging emotions and betrayals can linger and take time to heal. Just under half of women who had a partner or spouse who regularly viewed porn (46%) say they have fully recovered from the effects of this."[15] When any kind of betrayal occurs, including that caused by porn use, the brain begins to operate in a different way: the fear center fires up and remains hypervigilant, causing restlessness, anxiety, and a sense of being perpetually on guard.[16] This alters the brain's ability to regulate your mood, calm you, think and reason, and make intelligent decisions.

This kind of stress can cause inflammation, and chronic inflammation has been shown to cause chronic health conditions.

In a Q&A with Barna Group, Dr. Sheri Keffer said that her own research "revealed that 76% of the 100 betrayed partners surveyed showed clinical symptoms of post-traumatic stress."[17]

We'll talk about betrayal trauma in-depth later, but know that this is a common trait of any struggler—eventually, they cause trauma in those around them.

---

[15] Pure Desire Ministries, *Beyond the Porn Phenomenon*, 56.

[16] Kristin Beaufort, "Understanding the Ways Betrayal Trauma Alters the Mind & Body," Apr 29, 2022, *Bloom for Women*, **https://bloomforwomen.com/ways-betrayal-trauma-alters-the-mind-body-bt/**.

[17] Pure Desire Ministries, *Beyond the Porn Phenomenon*, 49.

We need a different way of considering sexual addiction.

Think of it this way—if someone struggling with a food addiction came into the church and asked for healing, we would pray over them for deliverance from whatever messages they were listening to or believing, pray about their compulsive need to eat, but we wouldn't expect them to walk out of the church 200 pounds lighter—that takes time. We would expect them to go home and change their eating habits, probably get into some kind of a support group, perhaps learn to cook differently, and change where they're buying their food.

We would expect freedom to come about as the end result of an entire process that involved many different aspects of their life.

All addictions affect us physiologically—that is, addictions are rooted in both our mind and our body. It's no different with sex addiction. Yes, there is power in prayer and confession. Jesus does create freedom in people's lives. But these things need to be lived out so the change that occurs isn't simply something temporary, but lasting. It takes time to find restoration, to return to the way of living and being that God originally intended.

2 Peter 1:3-5 has some encouragement that lines up with this:

> *3 His divine power has given us everything we need for a godly life through our knowledge of him who called us by his own glory and goodness. 4 Through these he has given us his very great and precious promises, so that through them you may participate in the divine nature, having escaped the corruption in the world caused by evil desires.*

[5] For this very reason, make every effort to add to your faith goodness; and to goodness, knowledge;

Do you see here how it is both/and? Yes, there are promises, and yes, God's divine power gives us everything we need to live godly lives … but also, Peter exhorts us to "make every effort" to go after goodness and knowledge. It's all of God and all of us, not one or the other.

We hope this is beginning to help you get a more accurate picture of those who struggle with sexual addiction and compulsive sexual behaviors—the common traits are not criminality or some kind of general moral erosion but have more to do with life circumstances, an unhealthy view of God, and an eroding inner health.

Perhaps one of the toughest things about these kinds of struggles is how they play on our natural identity.

After all, we are sexual beings.

CHAPTER THREE

WE ARE SEXUAL BEINGS

We are sexual beings.

There are many Christians out there who are uncomfortable with that sentence! We've heard the sermon or the youth group talk so many times that sex outside of marriage is dangerous, which led to many of us thinking all sex, even sex within marriage, was inherently dirty, certainly not something to be talked about in public. And because of that lack of conversation within the church about sex and sexuality, we're led to assume that's how it should be: sex isn't something we should talk about or ask about. It's a topic that makes people uncomfortable, so it's off-limits.

The danger in this is that we end up thinking it's probably not something God has much interest in, other than to tell us what not to do.

But we are sexual beings designed by God to have sex. God formed our physical bodies to experience pleasure—God knows and understands that we will pursue things that give us pleasure. If you have any doubt of that, read Song of Songs 7:8–9:

I said, "I will climb the palm tree; I will take hold of its fruit." May your breasts be like clusters of grapes on the vine, the fragrance of your breath like apples, and your mouth like the best wine.

God isn't bashful. In fact, sex was created by God and is part of the foundation of a happy marriage and family—it allows for a unique bond of intimacy between a married couple, and it can result in children, one of the building blocks of healthy communities and civilizations.

So we'll say it again: we were created to have sex. We were designed with a drive to have an intimate relationship with another person.

And yet there's an interesting dichotomy when it comes to sex, two sides to the same coin: sex can be wonderful, and, at the same time, sex can be destructive. Sex is like fire—in the right context, within the right conditions, it is a powerful force that can make life better. It can even help us to thrive. But, like an out-of-control wildfire, an unrestrained sex drive, an unmitigated pursuit of pleasure, can end up burning down everything in its path.

Can we take a minute and talk about the brain, the seat of the mind and ultimately the core of our desires? The truth is that our brain lies at the foundation of so much of our sexuality—what we want—and, as a result, the choices we make. The fact that God created us and our brains gives us a fascinating view into what we were created for, and what we were created to do.

The statement that we are sexual beings is supported by at least two main things: our bodies have been physically designed to have sex, and our minds were created and built in a way that reinforces sexual desire. Our sexual behavior, then, is impacted by a number of things, perhaps none more than the brain and how it operates.

So where do we begin?

It all really starts with the neurons in our brain and the connections between them—our brain has over a hundred billion neurons, and each one has at least 10,000 connections to other neurons, which means our brain, at any given time, is generating trillions of connections![18] These connections are electrical and chemical, played out by an electrical impulse traveling down the neuron and then shooting a chemical over to the receiving neuron.

As Heather Kolb would say, "This is where the human experience takes place."[19] The firing of these neurons keeps our hearts beating and our lungs breathing. They influence what our brain is taking in from our peripheral vision even when we're not conscious of it. It's what we smell, see, taste, touch, and hear, how we interpret that, and then what actions our bodies

[18] Herculano-Houzel S. "The human brain in numbers: a linearly scaled-up primate brain." *Front Hum Neurosci.* 2009;3:31. Published 2009 Nov 9. doi:10.3389/neuro.09.031.2009.

[19] The information in this chapter comes from our course, *Sexual Integrity 101*, presented by Heather Kolb. She's a professor, a mom, a wife, and an expert on neuroscience, and she has spent 20 years studying human behavior. In this particular session of the course, she walks us through the physical structure of the brain, and this will help us understand some of the why behind our behavior as well as what becomes addiction.

take in response to all that stimuli—all of it begins at the level of the neuron.

Every thought, feeling, sensation, and action originates in our brain with the firing of these neurons sending signals and chemicals between neurons. In fact, there's a saying in neuroscience that's important: "Neurons that fire together, wire together."[20] What this means is that as we repeat behaviors over and over and over again, those particular neural pathways in our brain become cemented together and make it even more likely that we will do that thing again. Whatever it is: waking up early, working out, memorizing information, brushing our teeth, having sex with our spouse, or looking at porn.

Neurons that fire together, wire together.

Repeat a behavior or a thought, and it becomes something you'll more than likely do again … which makes it even more likely you'll do it again. And again. And once we're in the habit of doing things—particularly those activities that bring us pleasure and light up the brain's reward center—our brain likes that, and continues to encourage it.

Our brain contributes to how this drive toward the repetitive reinforces sexual behaviors, both wanted and unwanted.

---

[20] Press Office, "How Neurons That Wire Together Fire Together," *NeuroscienceNews.Com*, December 23, 2021, **https://neurosciencenews.com/wire-fire-neurons-19835/**.

Then we move to the cerebral cortex, the exterior area of the brain, the part that looks like a giant walnut. While it's only three millimeters thick, it contains approximately 16 billion neurons.[21] This is where our higher processes take place: memory, thinking, learning, reasoning, problem-solving, emotions, consciousness, and sensory functions. It's what we refer to as our gray matter.[22]

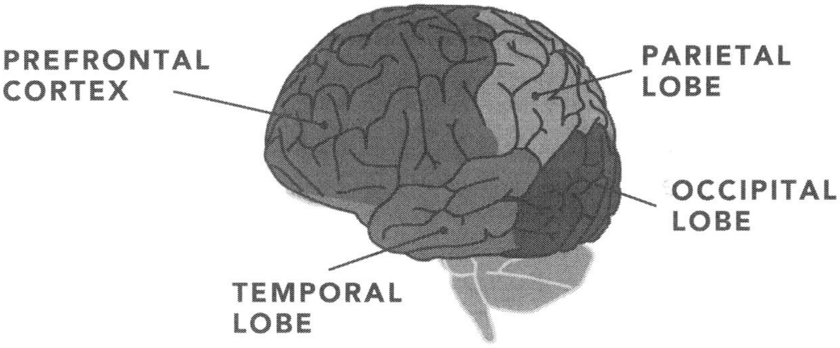

One part of the cerebral cortex is the prefrontal cortex, and it sits right behind our forehead. Now stay with us here—all this brain science is leading somewhere and we will connect the dots in a moment! The prefrontal cortex is the instrument of decision-making, planning, and impulse control, and it isn't fully developed until we're about 25 years old.[23] This is why young people will often make decisions or do things without any concern for potential results—the area of their brain in charge of decision-

[21] Tonya Hines, "Anatomy of the Brain," *Mayfield Brain & Spine*, April 2018, **https://mayfieldclinic.com/pe-anatbrain.htm**.

[22] Venkat S.R., "Cerebral Cortex: What to Know," *WebMD*, December 09, 2024, **https://www.webmd.com/brain/cerebral-cortex-what-to-know**.

[23] Arain M, Haque M, Johal L, et al. "Maturation of the adolescent brain." *Neuropsychiatr Dis Treat*. 2013;9:449-461. doi:10.2147/NDT.S39776.

making and impulse control hasn't even developed yet! They might look like young adults, but they still have baby brains.

We also have the parietal lobe, which helps us to regulate touch, temperature, pressure, and spatial awareness, along with the occipital lobe, at the very back, which helps us to interpret what our eyes are seeing.[24] When we see things, what's actually happening is that light enters the eye, goes through a neurological sequence, and is broken down into various forms of information: color, size, shape, dimension—basically anything we'd need to know about what we're seeing.

The human brain is very visual. In other words, what we think we see usually takes precedence, and those of us who aren't blind rely very much on our sight to fulfill many functions.

Because of this, we respond to visual sexual stimuli faster than anything else.

So, neurons that fire together wire together, reinforcing repetitive behaviors.

And visual stimuli cause our brains to respond.

Can you see how the function of our brains plays such a huge role in our sexuality, and especially in the things that we seek out to look at?

As a result of the brain's response to what we see, when someone is trapped in sexual addiction, their eyes basically become their own worst enemy, because the brain already craves visual input

---

[24] Mayo Clinic, "How Your Brain Works," July 02, 2024, **https://www.mayoclinic.org/diseases-conditions/epilepsy/in-depth/brain/**.

and responds faster to sexual stimuli than anything else. And we want to give the brain things it will respond to: when we watch porn, it lights up the brain, and those neurons wire together, create a strong connection, and make us want to do it again. And again. And again.

> *Pornography has the potential to change the structure and wiring in the brain tied to the reward system in ways similar to other addictive substances and behaviors ... Viewing pornography may make the brain become increasingly stimulated when the potential for porn is presented (potentially leading someone to crave porn) ... Those with these compulsive patterns also likely have less brain stimulation in the reward centers of the brain when watching porn, requiring longer viewing sessions to create the same rewards in the brain over time.*[25]

We'll talk more about addiction in the next chapter, but keep these things in mind when it comes to how porn can use our body's design against us.

---

[25] Brian Willoughby, "The Truths and Myths of Pornography Brain Research," *Ever Accountable*, **https://everaccountable.com/blog/the-truths-and-myths-of-pornography-brain-research/**.

Moving back to the structure of the brain, the temporal lobes of our brain have a right and left side—the right is for emotions, dreams, and music while the left is for analytical thinking, speech, and reason.[26] All are crucial in the development of empathy.

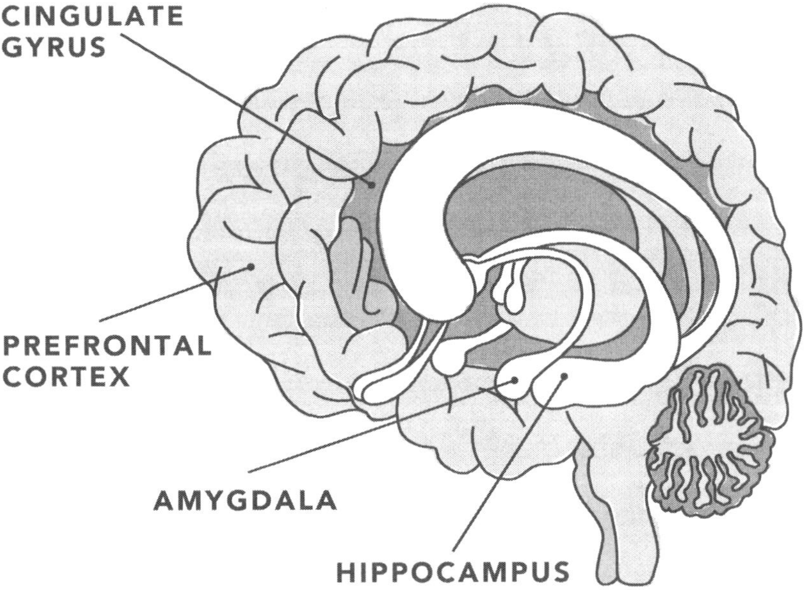

But now we're going to go deeper, into the very center of the brain, where our emotions and memory are controlled. This is called the limbic system, and it's an area of the brain that is very

---

[26] Tom Rush and Lana Burgess, "Left brain vs. right brain: Fact and fiction," *MedicalNewsToday*, November 22, 2023, **https://www.medicalnewstoday.com/articles/321037**.

sensitive to the neurotransmitter dopamine.[27] Our brain sends hundreds of billions of neural signals each second![28]

Did you catch that?

Hundreds of billions of neural signals are sent every second.

And many of these happen in the limbic system, the seat of emotion and memory. Have you seen the movie *Inside Out*?[29] The main character is a young girl named Riley, and her emotions are portrayed as individual beings doing their work at the very seat of her mind. They each take turns (or struggle with) having control over Riley's actions. The place where these emotions sit is kind of like the limbic system.

There are different parts that play a role in the limbic system: the main three we're focusing on are the prefrontal cortex,[30] which we've already talked about and which makes us uniquely human; the hippocampus, instrumental in moving memories from short-term to long-term (usually at night when we're sleeping); and

---

[27] Sanchari Sinha Dutta, "Limbic System and Motivation," *News-Medical*, Mar 10, 2021, **https://www.news-medical.net/health/Limbic-System-and-Motivation**.

[28] Salvatore Domenic Morgera, "How do brains tune in to one neural signal out of billions?," *The Conversation*, September 11, 2019, **https://theconversation.com/how-do-brains-tune-in-to-one-neural-signal-out-of-billions-121016**.

[29] *Inside Out*, directed by Pete Docter (Burbank, CA: Walt Disney Studios Motion Pictures, 2015), film.

[30] The prefrontal cortex is not part of the limbic system but receives information from the limbic system and is an important part of this neurological process.

the amygdala, the part of the brain that controls our emotions.[31] Anger. Sadness. But especially fear.

Especially fear.

When something happens in our environment that's out of our control, the amygdala activates.

The hippocampus and the amygdala work together—when something happens in our lives, the hippocampus draws in the details of that event and stores them, and the amygdala is going to capture how it made us feel in that moment. Those two things fuse together in our brain.

For example, if you were ever bit by a dog when you were a child, your hippocampus would remember everything about the event. The smells around you, the size and shape of the dog, who owned the dog, what was going on around you at the time. And then your amygdala would capture how that event made you feel—Alone? Unprotected? Afraid? Vulnerable to attack?

Years later, you might be approached by a dog and suddenly all of those feelings come rushing back because your brain had fused the details of the situation with a set of feelings—suddenly you see a dog and you panic, because feelings of fear, vulnerability, and an inability to protect yourself rush to the surface.

Imagine growing up in a home where someone was verbally abusive to you, shouting and screaming, often over something very small. And that made you feel afraid and vulnerable. Your

---

[31] Sanchari Sinha Dutta, "Limbic System and Motivation," *News-Medical*, Mar 10, 2021, **https://www.news-medical.net/health/Limbic-System-and-Motivation**.

brain is going to capture everything about that situation, from the smells around you to the color of the refrigerator and fuse that with those feelings, so that even years later some small detail can trigger the limbic system to raise the red flag.

The same could be said of sexual abuse.

The same can also be said of early sexual experiences where the brain is flooded with neurochemicals. The experience becomes locked into our way of responding to the world around us, whether we intended it or not.

Can you see how our brain influences our decisions around sexuality?

Can you see how it contributes to the things we choose to do, which become the things we choose to do over and over again, which soon become the very addictions we are drowning in?

There's another amazing thing about the brain.

It has a built-in drug dispenser.

It's called the VTA (ventral tegmental area).[32] It's the origin of the dopamine cycle, the natural reward pathway for the brain. The VTA is constantly on the lookout for excitement and novelty in our environment, and when it finds it, it gives our brain a huge hit of dopamine. This produces intense feelings of pleasure

---

[32] Julie A Kauer, "Addictive Drugs and Stress Trigger a Common Change at VTA Synapses," *Neuron*, Volume 37, Issue 4, February 20, 2003, Pages 549-550, ISSN 0896-6273, **https://doi.org/10.1016/S0896-6273(03)00087-4**.

and satisfaction. And God made us this way. He designed us to experience good and holy pleasure throughout our life. But this God-given design can easily be hijacked or confused.

There's a lab experiment where rats are given the opportunity to hit one of two levers—one delivers food, and the other delivers a hit of dopamine. So what's the more powerful motivator, food or dopamine?[33]

In many of these studies, the rats will hit the dopamine lever until they starve, preferring the hit of dopamine over the pleasure derived from eating. That's how strong the brain's craving is for dopamine. More, more, more.

Food increases the dopamine released in our brain by around 150%.[34]

The nicotine in cigarettes, when introduced into the blood and brain, increased dopamine production by 200%.

Sexual intercourse? This increases dopamine 250%.[35]

Our biological systems were designed to desire sex—it increases intimacy, gives us a sense of well-being, and helps lead to the continuation of human life.

---

[33] David Linden, *The Compass of Pleasure: How Our Brains Make Fatty Foods, Orgasm, Exercise, Marijuana, Generosity, Vodka, Learning, and Gambling Feel So Good* (New York: Penguin Books, 2011), 8-9.

[34] Alex DiFeliceantonio and Ashley N. Gearhardt, "Highly processed foods can share the addictive qualities of tobacco, researchers say," *Virginia Tech News*, 9 Nov 2022, **https://news.vt.edu/articles/2022/11/HPFsandtobacco_fralinbiomed_1109.html**.

[35] Relay Health Inc., "Can You Undo Years of Porn Addiction?," January 30, 2025, **https://www.joinrelay.app/blog/undo-porn-addiction**.

But anything that increases dopamine this much can also cause addiction. We see it with food. We see it with cigarettes. And we see it with sex … or acting out to pornography.

Now that we've taken a quick trip through the brain, can you see the two sides of the coin when it comes to sex?

On the one hand, these mechanisms of the brain can reward monogamous sexual behavior, create incredible intimacy between married partners, and solidify a bond that grows exponentially throughout someone's lifetime. One example of this is vasopressin. Vasopressin is a bonding hormone stimulated through physical and sexual behaviors.[36] It causes a male to become territorial, usually about their mate. It's called mate-guarding and was designed to help them bond specifically with their mate.

But it's also the same chemical that bonds a guy to an image or a specific fantasy when using porn. Watching porn reconditions their brain to respond to a specific set of stimuli, so when they get married, it may take time and intentionality to create a healthy sexual relationship with their wife, because their married sex life doesn't fit into what his brain has become reliant on in order to be aroused. Thankfully, there is a path to rewire our brains! This is one reason being in a group is important: it takes time to identify these areas, connect the dots, create a plan, and then

[36] C. Sue Carter and Allison M. Perkeybile, "The Monogamy Paradox: What Do Love and Sex Have to Do With It?," *Front. Ecol. Evol.*, 28 November 2018, *Sec. Behavioral and Evolutionary Ecology*, Volume 6 - 2018, **https://doi.org/10.3389/fevo.2018.00202**.

commit to the work, and the support of your group can help you get things back to the way they should be. It is not a lost cause! Our brains are incredible and capable of so much.

Meanwhile, hormones surge every month for women, contributing to sensitivity to emotional interactions such as approval or disapproval, acceptance and rejections. This can also become a time when women use masturbation as a self-soothing behavior. The limbic system is going to be affected by the surge of estrogen and progesterone, leading to more intense responses, especially to sex.[37] It also creates oxytocin, making her crave social bonding.[38]

These same mechanisms of the brain, when damaged or when we experience trauma, can reward thrill-seeking. We can become dopamine addicts, desperate for the next big sexual hit. Abuse paired with sex can lead to unhealthy or triggering feelings around sex—it can even end up linking pain with pleasure, which can be so confusing. Porn can become this thing our mind wants to feast on, over and over again.

Sex, something created as a natural and healthy part of who we are, can contribute to our wholeness or our destruction.

---

[37] Jennings KJ, de Lecea L. "Neural and Hormonal Control of Sexual Behavior." *Endocrinology*. 2020;161(10):bqaa150. doi:10.1210/endocr/bqaa150.

[38] Miranda Olff, et al., "The role of oxytocin in social bonding, stress regulation and mental health: An update on the moderating effects of context and interindividual differences," *Psychoneuroendocrinology*, Volume 38, Issue 9, 2013, Pages 1883-1894, ISSN 0306-4530, **https://doi.org/10.1016/j.psyneuen.2013.06.019**.

Once we understand how our brains have been hijacked, we then have the ability to look back and identify how we got to this point. Were there things we experienced in childhood that impacted the way we behave in relationships today? A key component of recovery is connecting the dots and reframing the thoughts we have associated with our feelings, which will ultimately change the way we behave.

So why do we struggle? And how can our experiences as children impact the way we view sex and sexuality?

CHAPTER FOUR

WHY DO WE STRUGGLE?

I (Ashley) was lonely growing up. By the time I was two, my parents divorced, and my mom was working long hours to provide for us. She grew up during tough times and desperately wanted to make sure her kids had what they needed. But because she was a single parent, this meant leaving us at home for long periods of time with babysitters. These babysitters were usually young, unhealthy women struggling in their own lives, with their own issues. Most of my childhood, I felt unwanted and alone.

I had sexual experiences with some of the babysitters' kids—they were confusing to my young mind, because I knew it was wrong. But it also awakened a curiosity about sex at a very young age. So there was the push-pull that Nick often talks about, the push of shame and the pull of curiosity. I didn't want to do those things because it made me feel dirty, but my natural curiosity often got the better of me.

In those days, when my mom got home from work, she was exhausted and would go straight to her room. Sometimes the babysitter would make us dinner; sometimes we had to fend for ourselves. Alone and uncertain without any foundation, I realized early in life that masturbation helped me escape my feelings of loneliness and allowed me to focus on something that made me feel good. My sexual curiosity was awakened at such a young age, but I didn't have anyone in my life to talk me through it or help me see what was happening.

Besides being a lonely kid, I also had to face life as a minority, and racial harassment started when I was 7. No matter where I went to school, no matter what environment I found myself in, I felt subhuman. Comments about my skin color became part of my everyday life, and those words cut deep into my soul, causing me to try to make up for my "shortcoming." Maybe if I was nice enough, giving enough, or sexually pleasing enough, someone would love me as much as they would if I were white.

At the age of 8, I fell in love with Jesus. My sister took me to church with her, and I immediately felt the love of Christ. I knew Jesus loved me. I could feel it! But I still longed to hear those words from another person, to be hugged and kissed and told how special I was. I wanted someone to want me. I craved intimacy and community and experienced a constant longing.

I started modeling at the age of 9 and quickly discovered that it might be the way to intimacy—my mother never missed a modeling opportunity, showing me that modeling was very important and worth showing up for. My appearance became my obsession, because even at 9, I was beginning to recognize that my looks might be the thing that drew people to me. This gave me what I had always wanted: the feelings (or illusion) of acceptance, intimacy, and even love. Maybe, if I looked the right way, I wouldn't be lonely anymore.

But the modeling industry, while showing me what I thought was a way to people's hearts, also cruelly and callously rejected me. In that industry, everything hinged on how you looked, and, more specifically, someone else's judgment of your looks. I was constantly being measured, and almost always being told I wasn't thin enough. At school I was teased and excluded because of my skin color. I was not accepted or wanted.

I couldn't figure out what I needed to do to feel like I belonged.

As I got older, I threw myself at anyone who showed interest, trying to escape my loneliness and low self-esteem. I became whoever I needed to be in order to fit in. When I was 15, I drank with older guys so they would think I was cool and let me hang out. I ended up getting raped.

I woke up feeling dirty and ashamed. I believed the godly man I dreamed of marrying would no longer want me. I felt disqualified from God's best. Looking back, this became a confusing crossroad for me because if I was honest with myself, it had actually felt good to be wanted and to have someone desire me.

I realized I could use my body and my sexuality as a weapon to get men to desire me. I felt more in control and less like a victim.

At the age of 16, I became friends with some Christian kids and returned to the church. I still loved Jesus but couldn't figure out how to live in the real world and honor Jesus at the same time. I threw myself into serving at church and recommitted my life to God, but when rumors of my past began trickling out, the walls to protect me from rejection shot back up.

I was tired of constantly worrying about being exposed for who I really was. I left the church and went back to my party friends. At least I didn't have to hide anything from this set of friends.

At 18, I got pregnant with twins. My biggest fears were my twins not knowing and loving God. I found a big church to hide in, married their dad (so I wouldn't be sinning) and tried everything in my power to make my Christian life "work" this time. When my unhealthy marriage ended, I took with me all of my feelings of failure, shame, worthlessness, and humiliation.

I decided that in order to take care of my twins, I would work harder than ever. I went back to school, worked three jobs, and graduated with a 4.0, but the stress got the better of me: I developed OCD, an eating disorder, and began a binge-purge cycle of over-serving in church and sleeping around. I was playing a sick game, trying to keep my problems buried. I cried out to God in my journals, desperately asking for help, direction, and wondering why He wouldn't save me from myself. I asked Him so many times to help me, yet I felt my whole life was a game of Whac-A-Mole and white-knuckling.

On the outside, I appeared to have it all together: I was a supervisor in a doctor's office, a devoted servant at church, and the mother of adorable twin boys who were well-provided for. But on the inside, I was still that little girl waiting for someone to love her unconditionally, but feeling too broken to believe I could ever have that.

Then I met a Christian man who also had a past, and I thought a relationship with someone like him would solve all my problems—a man is really what I wanted, and since he knew all about my past and still loved me, I didn't have to worry about having secrets. We got married, and it felt like the best thing that had ever happened to me.

But I missed all the signs that he, too, was unhealthy, and I was blinded by my desire for approval, intimacy, connection, and love. Neither of us knew what true intimacy looked like, and our marriage eroded. Then I discovered that my husband had been secretly struggling with a porn addiction.

The first person I felt truly loved me had betrayed me. He was a fraud, like everyone else. The feeling that my worth was based on my looks came rushing back, and I felt like that 9-year-old, rejected girl again.

How did I end up here again? I tried to do things right this time. How could I free myself from this cycle?

Hopefully you can recognize in the stories we told earlier about abuse and first encounters with pornography that the experiences we have as children around sex and sexuality often follow us long into our adulthood. Powerful chemicals in the brain fired through our neurons for the first time in those early experiences, and they became fused into our way of seeing the world sexually. Most of us carry these early experiences into our adulthood—and if we don't address them, they can lead to compulsive sexual behaviors that often turn into addictions, simply because of the way our pleasure-seeking brain works.

But these experiences around sex can be amplified when they're paired with sexual or other types of trauma. It is a well known reality that pain, fear, and risk all escalate our neurochemicals to even higher levels. So what's going on in our brains when we experience trauma? And how does that relate to our sexuality in our adulthood?

To explore this, we're going to take another short trip into the brain.

There's another area of the limbic system that we didn't talk about earlier, and it's called the cingulate gyrus—this is what links our motivation and our behavior, otherwise known as the gear-shifter of the brain.[39] In fact, it's the part that allows us to change our approach, be flexible and adaptable, especially when we recognize that our environment is changing.

But when we experience trauma, it makes us inflexible, and this area of the brain is also associated with obsessive and compulsive behaviors.

The entire limbic system is compromised by trauma. Trauma changes the way we think, feel, and respond. The hippocampus, in addition to what we mentioned earlier, serves as a natural watchtower in the brain telling us, "It's going to be okay. You're all right." Meanwhile, the amygdala is always pulsing for danger, on high alert, ready to make us aware of threats in our environment. Again, let's remember that this system was designed by God to keep us safe and to protect us from real danger in the world. But as we have already seen, these systems can also cause trauma and sexuality to become wired together.

If you step over an extension cord, your amygdala is screaming in your brain that it is a snake, but a healthy hippocampus will step in and say, *no, you're okay, that's just a cord.* If you're in the zoo at the lion enclosure, your amygdala is screaming that you'd better run because there's a lion right there. But your healthy

---

[39] Keith Rowe, "Anatomy of the Brain: How Well Do You Know Your Own Brain?," *BrainMD*, February 13, 2025, **https://brainmd.com/blog/anatomy-of-the-brain/**.

hippocampus steps in and says, *no, you're okay, that glass will keep you safe.*

When we experience trauma, our hippocampus decreases in size by up to 12%.[40] This means that trauma lessens our ability to reassure ourselves in stressful situations. If you've experienced sexual abuse or some other kind of trauma, you don't have as strong of a watchtower in your brain saying that you'll be okay. The trauma actually changes the formation of our brains.

But there's good news. These changes are not permanent. Or at least they don't have to be.

We can actually learn techniques that will help activate the hippocampus—things like writing poetry, journaling, or being creative. And while trauma can be debilitating, we're also learning through new neuroscience that even the most compulsive behavioral neural pathways can be rewired when we commit ourselves to a path of healing.

Even the strongest addictions can be undone.

Even the most ingrained compulsive sexual behaviors can be done away with.

The good news is that if trauma shaped the brain, healthy experiences of love and grace can reshape the brain!

An excellent example of the brain's ability to heal and reform strong neural pathways is a story about a college professor who was in his mid-60s when he suffered a massive stroke that

[40] Bremner JD. "Traumatic stress: effects on the brain." *Dialogues Clin Neurosci.* 2006;8(4):445-461. doi:10.31887/DCNS.2006.8.4/jbremner.

left him paralyzed.[41] He was, understandably, devastated. His entire life was changed, and his brain seemed to be permanently damaged. Most doctors and scientists back then didn't think the brain could heal itself once you reached a certain age—they thought the brain could only form large amounts of new neural connections when you were young, but that once you got older your brain was more or less set in its form.

Fortunately, the man's son was a neuroscientist, and he brought his dad back to his house and started working with him on basic movements. He taught him to roll over, to crawl, to feed himself, and even eventually to talk and to walk. He helped his dad recreate these movements until he could do them on his own—his brain just needed the repeated reinforcements in order to bring these movements back into his life.

Within a year's time that college professor was even back in front of the classroom teaching again! It was the beginning of our knowledge that the brain can heal, and that it can form new neural pathways even late in life.

Now, if after having his stroke he would have simply laid in bed and not put in the effort of movement, he never would have recovered. But because he had someone willing to help him retrain his brain, he was able to get back to a healthy, active life that very much resembled his life before the stroke.

Our brains want to be healthy. Our brains are capable of great change. But there's an intentionality that must take place if

[41] Norman Doidge, *The Brain that Changes Itself: Stories of Personal Triumph from the Frontiers of Brain Science* (New York: the Penguin Group, 2007), 20-26.

we're going to see healing in an organ as complex as the brain. We can't simply sit back and expect radical change.

There are some fascinating brain scans that illustrate this point. In one set of images, an individual's brain was damaged in the left prefrontal cortex—the left and right hemispheres of the brain have very different tasks and functions. But even so, in later scans of the same brain, you can see that the right side of the brain recognized something was wrong and began to pick up additional activity on the right side in order to compensate for the part of the brain that was damaged.

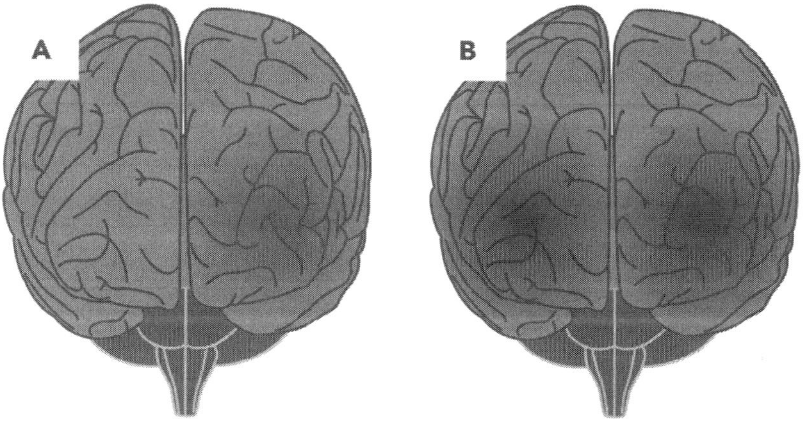

Our brains can rewire at incredible speeds—we can lay down new neural connections rapidly when we are intentional, when we put new things in place, when we develop tools and practices that will help us sustain health in our lives. But the key is intentionality.

Science journalist Sharon Begley writes, "The very structure of our brain, the relative size of the different regions, the strength of connections between them, even their functions reflect the lives we have led. Like sand on a beach, the brain bears the footprints of the decisions we have made, the skills we have learned, and the actions we have taken."[42]

Healing is possible. And in later chapters we'll begin to address the how-tos of healing, for the individual and the betrayed spouse, the couple, and the whole family.

While research and neuroplasticity show us that our brain is capable of great change, it's also the reason why our brain is vulnerable to our environment.

Dr. Patrick Carnes is a leading expert in sexual addiction, and after working with more than 660 patients he discovered that these are the common characteristics of those people who struggle with addictive behaviors—the impact of their family system and the abuse they experienced:[43]

- 87% of people who struggle with sexually addictive behavior had other addicts in their family
- 77% came from rigid family systems, or a home with strict rules but not much relationship

[42] Sharon Begley, *Train Your Mind, Change Your Brain: How a New Science Reveals Our Extraordinary Potential to Transform Our Lives* (New York: Ballentine Books, 2007), 8-9.

[43] Patrick Carnes, The Making of a Sex Addict, Adapted from "The Obsessive Shadow," 1998, **https://cdn.ymaws.com/iitap.com/resource/resmgr/arie_files/m1_article_the-making-of-a-s.pdf**.

- 87% came from a disengaged family system, or a home where not only was there not much relationship but there was also minimal parental contact
- 97% of those who struggle with sexually addictive behaviors came from an environment where they experienced some form of emotional abuse
- 81% experienced some form of sexual abuse
- 72% experienced some form of physical abuse

You can see how trauma affects the brain, and eventually it will even shape the kind of lives we live.

Year after year after year, I (Nick) experienced certain things that would trigger me to use porn or to go outside the guardrails of what was good for me and my sexuality. There were things that, even if I had been sober for a month or two or three, would bring me into a hard relapse. Things like getting on my phone without accountability software. Or watching television late at night on my own—things I knew I should avoid like the plague in my white-knuckle attempts at not going back to porn.

After all, porn had always been there for me when I was sad or angry or disappointed, when I was upset or felt rejected. Porn helped me escape the pain I felt, gave me some strange semblance of being accepted.

But what I started to notice a few years ago, after I'd been through the Pure Desire programs, was that I didn't even feel tempted by porn anymore. My knee-jerk reaction wasn't to check someone out or take a step away from sexual health—my knee-jerk reaction in times of pain or stress or disappointment was to text a friend, to reach out for support. The more I had these experiences of dealing with my pain in a healthy way, the more true satisfaction and happiness I felt.

It was amazing!

My brain had been rewired, and my responses to pain and loneliness and fear were completely different than they had been only a few years before. And this is a process that is ongoing today, and likely will be for the rest of my life! As Dr. Ted Roberts says, "We were all meant to be addicted to Jesus but we have learned to be addicted to other things."

There was no shame or guilt associated with these new ways of being. This further reinforced my transformation, to the point that, as I get further along in my journey, by the grace of God, I rarely even think about dealing with life in those ways anymore. It's almost like I never struggled with it, because I'm not walking through life trying to avoid this trigger or that trigger. I've got a new way of doing life, one that leads to true satisfaction.

This new way of life is available to all of us. Let's find out how.

PART TWO

THERE IS HOPE

CHAPTER FIVE

A WHOLE NEW WAY OF LIFE

Over the last few years, I (Nick) have two friends who have lost more than ninety pounds each. Combined, they've lost the equivalent of a human being my size! I'm amazed at what they've been able to do—when you see their before and after photos, and their before and after levels of health, what you see is a radical transformation. They are completely different people, not only because of the weight that they lost, but because they've changed mentally, emotionally, spiritually, and physically throughout the process.

Perhaps the most interesting part is that they each used completely different methods to lose this weight—it wasn't simply about eating less or exercising more. They both didn't give up dairy or sugar or embark on the same workout routines. Their journeys went beyond simply counting calories or running a certain number of miles every week—it required an entire transformation in how they approached life.

It's the same with all of us. If we want to really change, if we want to bring about incredible transformation, we can't just start or stop particular behaviors. We have to change our entire mindset! Whether we're talking about weight loss or other personal transformation stories, that's almost always the principle:

Lasting transformation is less about stopping or starting a specific behavior and more about adjusting how we do life.

This principle is particularly true in the area of our sexuality. If we want to eliminate our compulsive sexual behaviors, it's going to be about more than simply not doing something or introducing a new activity. We have to change the way we do life.

And this isn't just a problem for men. Seventy-five percent of Christian men and 40% of Christian women are viewing pornography.[44] Distorted ways of viewing and living out our sexuality is a people problem, one that affects so many.

In fact, research suggests that in 56% of divorces, it's the online behavior of one of the spouses that has driven the separation.[45] Compulsive sexual behavior is destroying lives and families. And many of us would agree. Many of us have been impacted by sexual brokenness, either in things we have done or in things that have been done to us.

But too often we have these compulsive sexual behaviors and we're stuck with the mindset we talked about in the introduction.

Is this it?

Maybe this is just how it's going to be.

---

[44] Pure Desire Ministries, *Beyond the Porn Phenomenon: Equipping the Church for a New Conversation about Pornography, Betrayal Trauma, and Healing* (Ventura: Barna Group, 2024), 6.

[45] Jill Manning, "The Impact of Internet Pornography on Marriage and the Family: A Review of the Research," *Sexual Addiction & Compulsivity*, 13:131–165, 2006.

I've tried to quit so many times—I just don't think I can do it.

My spouse keeps going back to that old behavior. They'll never change.

I think we all wonder if transformation is possible—true transformation, the kind that doesn't simply leave us doing new things, but becoming new people. New creations.

> *Therefore, if anyone is in Christ, the new creation has come: The old has gone, the new is here!*
>
> **2 CORINTHIANS 5:17**

If anyone is in Christ! The old? Gone. The new? Here.

Wouldn't that be wonderful? Wouldn't it be amazing if we could transform out of our old, destructive habits and into something fresh and new, something joyful and life-bringing? What if we could transform into people who weren't weighed down by our compulsive sexual behaviors? What if we could walk away from them and never look back?

The good news?

There is hope.

Every day at Pure Desire, we hear the stories of people who have come through, who can say, "I once was lost but now I'm found. I once lived in darkness and brokenness but now there's freedom and peace."

Transformation is possible.

Had you known me (Nick) at 30 when my friend helped me identify my porn addiction, you would have thought my life was perfect, or close to it. I led a thriving, young church full of hard-working folks who looked up to me and believed in our vision. I was married to a beautiful wife, a woman I was completely in love with and who was completely in love with me. We had three incredible children together, and I was successfully coaching track at a nearby school. Everything in my life—from the outside—looked to be trending up.

But behind the scenes? My marriage was on the verge of disaster and collapse. The distorted view of sex I had developed as a child due to early exposure had led me to a lifelong binge-purge relationship with porn. I would binge on it, and the resulting shame and regret led me to purge it from my life … but only for a time, until one of my triggers had me back in the binge cycle. It was killing me on the inside, driving me deeper and deeper into darkness, and destroying my relationship with my wife.

After innumerable conversations where I would confess and promise I would change, only to fall back into it, my wife was at a breaking point.

"Nick, I love you," she finally said one day. "But I don't love the pain you're causing me. And since I don't know if the pain will ever change, I don't know if I can stay."

My wife didn't know if she could stay? Everything I cared about the most was in jeopardy, simply because of this compulsive sexual behavior: my habitual use of porn. That conversation brought everything to the surface, including all the lies I had been telling myself for so long, the ways I had convinced myself that what I was doing wasn't a big deal.

I'm working on it.

It's only once in a while.

It's going to get better.

It's not hurting anyone.

This is the last time–I promise.

But I hadn't been able to stop, my wife was on the verge of leaving, and I hated myself for it.

How can we bring about lasting change in our lives?

As I mentioned earlier, true transformation isn't about stopping or starting a particular behavior—that's only what we see or experience on the surface. Transforming from someone addicted to pornography or soliciting prostitutes or sleeping around can't be addressed by simply turning off the computer or getting another piece of software on the laptop or never leaving the house.

True transformation only comes about by changing the way we do life.

But I didn't know all this at the time. My initial attempts at escaping the clutches of pornography involved building the boundary walls of my life so high that porn could no longer find its way in. I decided I would be safe. I would get the best website blockers and accountability software. I wouldn't watch television alone. I'd limit the sites I could visit on my phone. I would effectively do everything in my power to keep porn out.

Here's the thing: I thought the problem was out there, when in truth the struggle was actually inside of me. I could build those walls as high as I wanted, but if nothing changed on the inside, it was only a matter of time before I was in the wrong place with the wrong attitude and the wrong motivations, and I would do the same old things all over again. I knew the pattern. Changing my outward circumstances wouldn't be enough.

Quite frankly, this vulnerability scared me to death. It started to feel like there might actually be no way out.

That's when I discovered Pure Desire Ministries, and my wife and I decided to give it a try, me as the one struggling and my wife as the one who had been betrayed. In groups and counseling we began to understand that there were deeper things driving my behavior than simply a desire to watch porn. All that time, I had thought porn was the problem, but porn was just a symptom of much deeper problems: for example, my attempts at finding my identity in success and popularity, which, when unmet, led to using porn as a way of medicating my brokenness.

Going through the Pure Desire program, which we'll talk more about later, was like coming out of a fog, waking up for the first time in my life. I quit hiding things, stopped lying, and perhaps most importantly stopped trying to convince everyone (including myself) that all was well. I owned my actions and found ways to support my wife so she could heal from the pain I had caused.

"I finally feel like I have my husband back," my wife said.

We still refer to the timeline of our marriage as "before Pure Desire" and "after Pure Desire." The people we are and the marriage we have is night-and-day different.

It was a complete and radical transformation.

Soon we realized God was telling us that our story wasn't just for us. This freedom we had found? Others needed it, too, and we could share the path with them.

I first had to get over my own hesitation. When my wife and I walked through this year-long journey, my initial desire was to get healthy, change behaviors, and move on with my life and ministry, never to talk about this again. But in one of my final counseling sessions, Dr. Ted Roberts challenged me, "Nick, if you keep silent about your story, what will happen to all the men and women in your church who are also struggling? Is your healing only for you?"

It was then that my spiritual coach helped me realize the first step to this was coming clean with my own church, telling them what I had been struggling with and explaining the path my wife and I had taken to wholeness and healing. He warned me that what some people really want is a perfect pastor, someone who has it all figured out, and if I get vulnerable and real, people might leave our church.

But I felt that we had to share our story. Others were trapped, and I couldn't keep silent about the hope and healing we had discovered. So, we did.

At a weekend service, I stood up in front of the church and disclosed this struggle I had with porn ever since I was a kid, the long road my wife and I had been on, and the freedom I had found. I asked for my church's forgiveness for failing them as a leader in this area, for not modeling what I was preaching, and I asked for their help to start a ministry in the church for men and women battling compulsive sexual behaviors.

Remember how I had been warned that people would be turned off, that people would leave? We experienced the complete opposite—rather than leaving, people leaned in. They came up to me after the service with tears in their eyes and said, "If it's safe for you to have this story and be our pastor, then I know it's safe for me to face my story, too."

So, how can this kind of transformation take place in our sexuality?

How can we experience lasting change—not having just a good month, or a few small wins, but radical transformation?

The Bible tells us of a man named Paul who traveled the world starting churches. Only a few years earlier, he had been one of the primary persecutors of early Christians, but after an amazing transformation (you can read about it in Acts 9), he found himself on the side he had once hated, leading people to Christ and encouraging small communities of believers as they were being formed.

In Paul's letter to the Roman church, he is trying to help them understand all that God is doing in them and in the body of Christ. Toward the end of the letter, in Romans 11:33–36 (NLT), he writes,

> 33 *Oh, how great are God's riches and wisdom and knowledge! How impossible it is for us to understand his decisions and his ways!*
>
> 34 *For who can know the Lord's thoughts?*
> *Who knows enough to give him advice?*
> 35 *And who has given him so much*
> *that he needs to pay it back?*
>
> 36 *For everything comes from him and exists by his power and is intended for his glory. All glory to him forever! Amen.*

Basically, Paul is saying that God is so immense, so awesome, and so wonderful that there's nothing we can give to Him … and yet He has chosen to give so much to us. God is so knowledgeable and incredible that we can't even begin to fathom the depth of God's thoughts. Everything comes from Him, exists by His power, and exists for His glory.

Everything comes from God.

Think about that for a minute—"Everything" is an all-encompassing word.

Nature exists for God's power and glory.

The church exists for God's power and glory.

Our sexuality exists for God's power and glory.

Wait … our sexuality exists for God's power and glory?

Too many people have created a dangerous divide between their spirituality and their sexuality. We have God and Jesus and faith and the Bible over on one side, and those things are holy and good and we're supposed to talk about them … and then we have our sexuality on the other side, something that's borderline unclean, and definitely not something we're supposed to talk about. We think that God doesn't have too much to say about our sexuality—maybe He's even embarrassed by it (we certainly are much of the time)—so we really shouldn't bring it up. Maybe we even pretend it doesn't exist.

Some of us don't know how to wrap our brains around the idea that God could somehow be intimately involved in our sexuality, that He created each of us that way, and that He cares about the way sex and our sexuality exist in each of our lives. Many of us can't comprehend God in this way. Instead, we feel like God is a dictator who wants to keep us down, make us good little boys and girls who are forced to obey Him. We need to do what He says and never act outside the lines. If we stay in a safe, small box, then He will love us. He certainly doesn't know what to do with sex and sexuality.

The truth is, God made you—including your sexuality.

The truth is, God has a good plan for you—including your sexuality.

His plan is goodness and freedom and joy—it's so much better than any of us have been led to believe.

This is where we have to begin, with this belief that God made us and has a good plan, a plan of freedom and joy and goodness, even for our sexuality, and that if we have compulsive sexual behaviors, radical transformation is possible.

Can you recognize His goodness?

Do you believe that He's for you?

That He's not trying to keep something from you or get something from you, but that God has something to give you in this area of your sexuality?

If we can start with this foundation of understanding and believing God has a good plan for our sexuality, then we're ready for true transformation.

And Paul shows us the path.

When we believe that everything comes from God, including our sexuality, we can bring this area of our life completely to Him. Rather than hiding or ignoring this shameful secret, we can embrace the truth that God loves us as we are and wants us to bring everything to Him. When we do, when we quit trying to just stop a behavior and instead look for a new way of doing life, transformation can occur!

CHAPTER SIX

THE PATH TO TRANSFORMATION

In the days when Paul was writing, there was a common practice in Israel, and that practice was sacrificing. At different points throughout the year, people brought some of their harvest of olive oil or grain or maybe even the very best of their livestock to a physical altar, laid it there with the help of a priest, and gave it up. In this act of sacrifice, they were saying, "This now belongs to you, God, not to me. I could have kept this for myself, but I'm giving it to You."

Imagine you're hungry and scrambling to find food every day. How difficult would it have been to put that handful of grain into the fire, knowing it would have helped you feed your family? It was the kind of sacrifice that really cost something.

Imagine one of your children is about to get married and you'll soon be hosting the wedding feast, and yet you have to leave your only lamb with the priests in order to be slaughtered. That definitely wouldn't have been an easy thing to do.

That's the whole point of a sacrifice—it isn't simple. It doesn't come naturally.

Paul is tapping into this difficult process of sacrificing when he writes his letter to the Romans:

And so, dear brothers and sisters, I plead with you to give your bodies to God because of all he has done for you. ***Let them be a living and holy sacrifice****—the kind he will find acceptable. This is truly the way to worship him.*

ROMANS 12:1 (NLT)

They understood physical sacrifices back then—they knew what it was like to give up something physical, something tangible, as a testament to God.

But their actual bodies? What was Paul talking about when he spoke of giving their bodies as a sacrifice? The concept was familiar to them … but sacrificing their own bodies? That would have gotten their attention.

The good part is that Paul isn't pleading for physical death. He's not arguing that our physical bodies have to die in order to follow God. Instead, he says this is a living sacrifice, but it's the same idea: we are asked to give our bodies to God.

What does that even mean?

How can you give something as a living sacrifice?

When Paul pleads with us to consider offering our bodies in this way, what he's really asking us to think about is who is calling the shots. Who's in charge? Are we living the way we want to live, or are we living the way God wants us to live?

And for us today, we're being challenged to ask, *Who's calling the shots with my sexuality?*

Am I? Or is God?

We will either do what is most pleasurable and satisfying in our own eyes, doing things our own way, or we'll allow God to direct us. We'll seek out what God wants us to do, and then do it. We'll give up our own opinions and desires, and we'll allow God to show us the best way.

Notice that Paul is pleading with his audience. "I *plead* with you to give your bodies to God." He understands that this doesn't come naturally to us—the natural thing to do is what we talked about in the earlier chapter about our status as sexual beings. Our human nature is to hold on and to pursue self-driven pleasure … only to discover, sooner or later, that this path has become the avenue of our own destruction.

He also understands what's at stake. If we do whatever we want when it comes to our bodies, the results will be disastrous, leading to conflict, disappointment, shame, destruction, and death (often the death of relationships and sometimes even physical death).

The stakes are high, so Paul pleads. He begs. He says that if we want to worship God—this God who has a good plan for us—and if we want to stay within the bounds of that good plan, we worship God by allowing God to call the shots.

What does that look like?

Well, Paul begins by telling us what it *doesn't* look like: conforming to the way of the world.

As we consider that word "conforming," let's go on a little trip into word meaning.

Imagine, for a minute, the molds that are used to create things, molds that help plastic or metal take on and hold its shape as it becomes something new. Maybe it's something as small as the plastic G.I. Joe action figures or Barbie dolls we played with as children, or something as large as steel being poured into molds that will eventually become beams that hold up skyscrapers. The molds that these substances are poured into determine the shape of the new, transformed thing. If molten steel is poured into a mold the shape of a circle, or if it's simply poured out onto the ground, it won't take the shape of a beam! It must be poured into the mold, where it will harden and become useful in that way.

This is precisely the image Paul is going for in the next verse as he pleads that we give our bodies to God as living sacrifices:

> ***Don't copy the behavior and customs of this world,*** *but let God transform you into a new person by changing the way you think. Then you will learn to know God's will for you, which is good and pleasing and perfect.*
>
> ROMANS 12:2 (NLT, EMPHASIS ADDED)

The word picture here behind the original word used for "copy" is a mold where clay or wax is pressed down and shaped to look a certain way. That's the image Paul wants his readers to envision—don't copy the ways of the world.

Don't be pressed into a mold that makes you look or behave exactly like everyone else.

Do not be conformed.

Do not be pressed into doing things the way the world does them.

Nearly everything we know and believe about our sexuality has been influenced by the culture around us. Even when we're not aware of it, there's a mold we're being pressed into, a mold we don't even think about. This can be positive or negative.

If you've grown up around a lot of people who have gone to college, it's more likely that you'll form in that way, that you'll be pressed into the "mold" of becoming a college student. But if you've grown up around people who started their own businesses or worked in the trades right out of high school, it's likely that "mold" of life will be the one you find yourself being formed into.

If you spend time in high school or college with other teenagers who drink or do drugs, then it's very likely you'll be pressed into the mold of that lifestyle. But if you surround yourself with other teenagers who don't do those things, then it's probable you'll be formed in that way.

Far too many of us have never paused to question some of the sexual assumptions or the ways we think about our sexuality, and how our culture has formed us and our minds around these topics. We've been pressed into our world's mold of sexuality, and we've never even thought about it or noticed it! We never ask ourselves,

- *Why do I think this is true about sex and sexuality?*
- *Where did that idea about sex come from?*
- *Is that view of sexuality accurate?*

There are (at least) seven ways our culture tries to press us into the mold of its own version of sexuality. As we go through each of them, consider which you have taken on and believed. Pause and think about each one. Are they true for you? And if you find that you've been pressed into these molds, consider how the belief or beliefs have affected the way you live and view your own sexuality.

Sex equals identity. In other words, the true measure of who I am is how much sex I have or how sexually appealing I am to others. The idea is that if I lack those things, if I'm not having sex or being sexually appealing, somehow, this makes me less valuable or important than others. If we're having a lot of sex or are sexually attractive, then we're better than those who aren't.

Where did this idea come from?

Do you believe it to be true, perhaps even subconsciously? If so, how has this belief—this mold—impacted your life?

It's so far from the truth. Our identity and value don't come from sex. Not even close! Our identity and value come from being children of God, created by God in the Divine image, having been made by God and loved by God. This is our identity.

Have you been pressed into the mold, conforming to this way of viewing yourself and those around you?

If so, how does this affect the way you value yourself and others?

What if you stopped believing this lie and began reminding yourself that true value is inherent in all humans, created and loved by God?

I can't help what I feel. There's this pervasive notion that we can't help what we feel, what we're drawn to, or what we desire. This is simply a biological occurrence that should be followed. The world tells us that any and every desire should be followed, experienced, and indulged. If it feels good, do it.

The truth is that what we feel and desire is a unique and powerful combination of our nature (the way we were created) and our nurture (the influence of the world around us). Our family of origin, the culture we grew up in, our way of life as children, and the experiences we've had—both things we've done and things others have done to us—have a deep influence and, to a degree, dictate how we feel about our sexuality.

Your brain has been shaped in particular ways based on your experiences. The good news is that your brain can be reshaped. You may feel like you can't help it, but, thankfully, the good news is that transformation is possible and you *can* help what you feel.

Everyone else is doing it.

It's a guy thing.

That's just how girls are.

Everyone our age is doing it.

At least I'm not having sex.

When we were teens, we thought in this juvenile way. As we mature and learn more, we need to be intentional about identifying our go-to excuses so we can change the pattern. Because if we don't, our brains will rationalize with us that everyone is doing it, so it can't be that bad.

If all of our friends are looking at porn, what could be so bad about it?

If all of our friends are sleeping around, then it's just the way the world is, right?

If everyone else struggles with compulsive sexual behaviors, then I should just stop feeling guilty about it, right?

It's just not true.

Whether or not everyone else is doing something is such a low standard of how to live and how to make choices. For those of us who have been called not to conform but to be transformed, we have to ignore this kind of rationalization. Examine your sexuality, and think through what you're doing—not in the light of what everyone else is doing—but in the light of God's Word, love, and plan for your life.

And then decide accordingly.

I will always struggle. This one is very similar to number three—if everyone else is struggling with something, whether it's eating too much sugar or watching porn, it's easy for us to justify doing that thing ourselves. And then we quickly say that since everyone else is struggling, I'll always struggle too. Obviously if my friends can't stop, I'll never be able to either. Why should I even try?

What's behind this idea when it comes to our sexuality is that our sexuality is actually stronger than we are! My desires will always be greater than my ability to change ... or so goes the mold we're being pressed into. Rather than looking for complete freedom, we decide to try to manage the behavior, keep it within certain parameters.

We underestimate our own ability to change, to break out of the mold we've been pressed into.

Don't listen to the lie that says you will always struggle. Complete freedom is possible.

I must have a sexual outlet. The fifth way we're pressed to conform is with this idea that we must have a sexual outlet, that sexually expressing ourselves is necessary when it comes to being human. Maybe this pokes and prods with your paradigms a bit, and we did write earlier that being sexual is a human condition, but have you ever considered the fact that if you don't have sex, you won't die?

If you don't have a personal, private release through masturbation, your body won't shut down.

Sex is not a necessity for life, but we've been led to believe it is.

How would you see your life differently if you could get out of this mold, this way of thinking?

No one is being hurt. Yet another way we've been pressed into our culture's way of thinking is through the idea that when it comes to our own personal sexuality, we can do whatever we want because in most cases no one else is being hurt by what we're doing. Pornography use has been presented to us as a victimless, harmless act. We can watch porn because we're not actually engaging in sexual acts, so who could we possibly be hurting? We can entertain fantasies because they're only in our mind—how is this hurting anyone? We can even sleep around because, hey, we're all consenting adults, right? And no one is being hurt.

This is a lie we go on believing right until the point when someone is hurt.

The people being exploited in an industry we actually know very little about.

The affair.

The abuse of a child.

The stories we don't like to tell.

What we find at Pure Desire in the stories told to us is that our deepest pain is often sexual in nature, and this is because the truth about sexuality is being hidden from most of us. The lie says no one is being hurt, even though the truth is that our compulsive sexual behaviors are hurting us ... even when done in secret, even if no one else knows about them!

These secret behaviors that "aren't hurting anyone" are actually setting us up for poor future relationships. They're weakening the intimacy between us and our partner. They cause us to distance ourselves from God and others. They negatively affect the way we think about ourselves. And often they change what is required to arouse us, leading us further away from our spouse—the design God had in mind for us—and even into physical changes like erectile dysfunction, becoming dependent on the behavior, or contracting sexually transmitted diseases. The stark truth is that pornography use is hurting us—the one who uses it! This should cause us pause, even before we consider if it hurts others (which it does).

These secret behaviors are causing damage and destruction, and rather than avoiding the truth and telling ourselves, "This isn't hurting anyone," we need to deal with it, face them head on, and experience radical transformation.

More sex equals a better life. The seventh way we're being conformed to this world is the belief that those who are having more sex are somehow enjoying more life, when the reality is that so many people are pursuing an empty, false hope and promise. The culture insists that sex always delivers, but in many cases and scenarios, sex can actually leave us wanting more, feeling lonelier, and never experiencing satisfaction.

More sex is not the measure of being relationally fulfilled.

In fact, it can actually be the opposite.

More sex might just be the act of a desperate person trying to find intimacy somewhere in the world.

Or more sex might be an outward sign of an inward struggle for worth and value and significance.

More sex doesn't mean a better life.

Don't be pressed into the mold of sexuality that the world tries to force us into. There are so many things about this way of viewing sex and our sexuality that are damaging and unhealthy and put us on a road that takes so much work to recover.

Hopefully by now you're wondering that if that's the mold we should avoid, what's the mold we should be pressed into? How should we view our sexuality? What is the true path to healing, wholeness, and transformation when it comes to our sexuality?

We're glad you asked!

Because it's the second part of Paul's verse, the same one we just looked at, where he gives us the answer.

> *Don't copy the behavior and customs of this world,* ***but let God transform you into a new person by changing the way you think****. Then you will learn to know God's will for you, which is good and pleasing and perfect.*
>
> ROMANS 12:2 (NLT, EMPHASIS ADDED)

"But let God transform you into a new person by changing the way that you think."

Changing the way we think—not the way we behave—is the key to long-lasting, permanent, and beautiful transformation. The patterns and the lies and all the things that have become part of the way we do life have to change. We have to break the molds we've been pressed into and let God transform us with His way.

We want to invite you into this new way of thinking—it's a process that takes time, not something that can be done in an instant. It's nearly impossible to sit down and say, "Okay, now I'm going to think differently." The reality is that our patterns of thinking have been shaped and created over an entire lifetime of decisions, emotions, and experiences. Addiction researchers are saying that lasting change is a three to five-year process![46] It takes time!

But it's an experience that Paul is inviting us into, because as we renew our thinking, we can radically transform our way of living.

The real hope of what Paul is saying is found at the end of the Scripture.

> *Don't copy the behavior and customs of this world, but let God transform you into a new person by changing the way you think.* ***Then you will learn to know God's will for you, which is good and pleasing and perfect.***
>
> ROMANS 12:2 (NLT, EMPHASIS ADDED)

---

[46] Patrick Carnes, *Task-Centered, Competency-Based Approach to Treatment*, 1998, **https://cdn.ymaws.com/iitap.com/resource/resmgr/arie_files/m1_article_task-centered-com.pdf**.

Then you will know God's good, perfect, and pleasing will for you. Knowing the goodness of God's plan often comes after we commit ourselves to a new way of thinking. We can't see it until we begin to live it.

Then you'll know what to do.

You'll know the mold you should be pressed into.

You'll know the true essence of your sexuality.

Maybe you have some compulsive sexual behaviors, but just the thought of trying to climb your way out of that mess doesn't sound good, perfect, or pleasing. Maybe the path ahead doesn't seem that wonderful. Maybe you're afraid of what others will think, what your closest friends might say, or how your spouse will respond to the truth.

Paul promises that if we remove ourselves from the customs of the world—if we refuse to be placed in that mold any longer—our thinking will be transformed, and we'll know what to do. The lure of society and what it portrays in regard to our sexuality can seem like the better way. But what God has for us is so far beyond what we could ask or imagine.

We can experience a radical transformation of our sexuality, and it's tied to walking in God's way. The life-giving plan becomes evident as we walk. But we have to be willing to offer our body as a living sacrifice, believe God's plan is good, and not get pressed into this cultural mold, this cultural way of being.

So where does this transformation begin?

Where do we start?

Once again, Paul points the way, this time in verses 3, 4 and 5:

> *Because of the privilege and authority God has given me, I give each of you this warning: Don't think you are better than you really are. Be honest in your evaluation of yourselves, measuring yourselves by the faith God has given us.* [4] *Just as our bodies have many parts and each part has a special function,* [5] *so it is with Christ's body. We are many parts of one body, and* ***we all belong to each other****.*
>
> **ROMANS 12:3-5 (NLT)**

There's no mistaking it.

What Paul calls us to is **community.** When it comes to walking in the transformed life of godly sexuality, it begins by humbling ourselves and entering into community. To spend time with others who can say, "Me, too. You're not alone." The lie our world tells us is this is too embarrassing to talk about, our sexuality and the mistakes we've made are too shameful, and each one of us is the only one struggling.

But that's just not the case.

You don't have to do this on your own.

We all belong to each other.

CHAPTER SEVEN
THE ESSENTIAL COMMUNITY

If you ever go to a Liverpool soccer game in Liverpool, England, you'll witness one of the most incredible things to ever happen in the sports world. It's a city of just under half a million people on the west coast of England, on the shore of an estuary that leads to the Irish Sea. It has been an important port city during its history, something that has given those who live there the reputation of being tough, blue collar, and no nonsense.

The fans of the Liverpool soccer team are dedicated and enthusiastic, and why not? Liverpool FC is "the most successful English team in European football tournament history, having won six European Cup/Champions League trophies and has also won the English top-division league title 19 times."[47] It was a decidedly industrial city during the Industrial Revolution, and there are still roots of this in the factories and warehouses that line the river.

But it's not their "footballing" success or their history that's remarkable. It's what happens before each and every soccer game that's rather incredible.

---

[47] Clive Gifford, "Liverpool Football Club," *Encyclopedia Britannica*, May 30, 2025, **https://www.britannica.com/topic/Liverpool-FC**.

After the teams are introduced, and before the game officially begins, a song starts playing over the loudspeaker. At this point, every Liverpool FC fan in the stadium (which seats 61,276 people) stops what they're doing, stands to their feet, and holds their bright red Liverpool scarf up with two hands. Many of them, even strangers, put their arms around each other's shoulders. These are tough-looking "blokes," men and women who are used to the rain and the cold, who work hard for a living. It's the third most deprived locality in England, with "63% of residents living in areas ranked among the most deprived in England, and 3 in 10 children living in poverty."[48]

But when the music starts, they lift their faces to the sky.

And they start singing.

When you walk through a storm
Hold your head up high
And don't be afraid of the dark

At the end of a storm
There's a golden sky
And the sweet silver song of a lark

Walk on through the wind
Walk on through the rain

[48] Melanie Harvey, "Stark report outlines health challenges in Liverpool by 2040 and the actions needed to tackle them," *Liverpool Health Partners*, November 1, 2024, **https://liverpoolhealthpartners.org.uk/stark-report-outlines-health-challenges-in-liverpool-by-2040-and-the-actions-needed-to-tackle-them/**.

For your dreams be tossed and blown

Walk on, walk on
With hope in your heart
And you'll never walk alone

You'll never walk alone

Walk on, walk on
With hope in your heart
And you'll never walk alone

You'll never walk alone[49]

Their voices rise in a stunning sound that reverberates through the stadium. Some of them close their eyes, while others get noticeably tearful. They sing as loud as they can, their voices drowning out the music. The players stand and wait on the field for the song to conclude.

When the last line comes, anyone who wasn't previously singing raises their voice. It's deafening.

"You'll never walk alone."

It's incredibly powerful.

But it has a deeper meaning, too. After the 1989 Hillsborough disaster, when ninety-six football fans lost their lives, the song's lyrics offered comfort, but also determination—"walk on

[49] Rodgers & Hammerstein, "You'll Never Walk Alone," *Carousel*, 1945, **https://breakingcharacter.com/youll-never-walk-alone/**.

through the wind," it urges, "walk on through the rain … and you'll never walk alone." This is a city that refused to back down in the face of establishment cover-ups and calls to "move on."[50]

Often, when we're in the midst of tragedy, hardship, or struggle, we need community around us more than ever. If we can see this truth being lived out by 60,000 soccer fans in England, how much more might this truth relate to our need for community and support in the recovery process?

Maybe you heard this a lot, too, when you were a child: "If you don't have anything nice to say, don't say it at all."

This idea can seep deep into our self-conscience, eventually dominating the way we interact as adults. Without even realizing it, we get to a place where we don't even want to disclose bad things about ourselves, simply because it's not nice. We think it's probably better off if we stay quiet.

But it's a lie we have to face and overcome because being honest breaks the cycle of shame in our lives.

In the book *Setting Us Free,* I (Nick) talk about the Shame Cycle, how when we sin, we feel a level of guilt or shame. Guilt is a feeling we experience when we have done bad. But shame is another step entirely, causing us to feel that we are bad. The only

[50] Tim Jonze, "How You'll Never Walk Alone came to define Liverpool FC's spirit," *The Guardian*, January 4, 2021, **https://www.theguardian.com/music/2021/jan/04/how-youll-never-walk-alone-came-to-define-liverpool-fc-spirit-gerry-marsden**.

other option is secrecy, but that leads us to isolation, eventually creating separation between God, us, and others. When we're lonely and separated, this cycle of shame pulls us down even deeper, increasing the likelihood that we will continue to go back to the very behavior we want to change.

We do something bad, think we are bad, and decide not to tell anyone. The secrecy leads to isolation, which often leads us back into bad behavior.

And on, and on, and on.

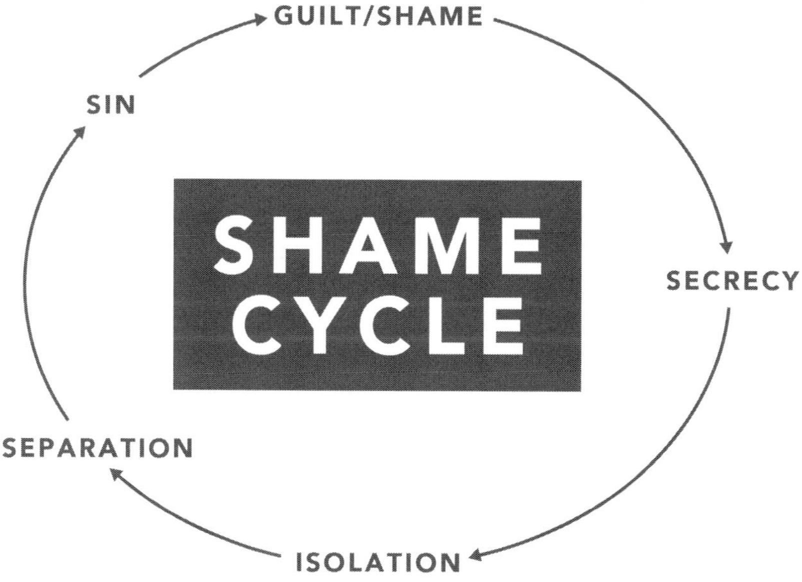

Whenever we sin, we can either face the pain or avoid the pain. Telling the truth about ourselves and our lives will be painful, no doubt. And for most of us, we've lived our lives free of this pain. And why not? Our culture encourages us to do anything possible to avoid pain—why would we willingly go into it? Pain avoidance, however, is at the root of our struggle with compulsive sexual behavior.

But you can choose to face the pain and embrace God's truth that this kind of pain is for your good because it will transform you in a way nothing else can. Facing the pain means choosing to be honest. To tell the truth. And it's not easy.

But by being honest, we let God and others in, and we open ourselves up to the possibility of receiving forgiveness, where we can hear those we love, and even God, telling us they don't hold this against us any longer.

In this forgiveness, we can experience true intimacy—not something that's the result of earning or proving we're worthy, but the result of being fully known and still loved and accepted. There's nothing else to prove, nothing else to do, nothing else to check off the list—there is only the freedom of being known and accepted for who we truly are.

This culminates in an intimacy leading to communion with God and others.

This is what we're longing for most: a sense of true community.

When you break out of the shame cycle by telling the truth, you enter a right relationship with God and others, something that fills up the places of deep need in your life. Your addictions no longer have the same pull they had before because what you were longing for is being fulfilled by God! In addiction or compulsive sexual behavior, we run away from relationship with God and others, and like Adam and Eve, end up in hiding. In a journey of healing, we discover that relationship with God and others is actually what we need most. When we face the challenges of life with others, we no longer need the coping behaviors that drive our struggle.

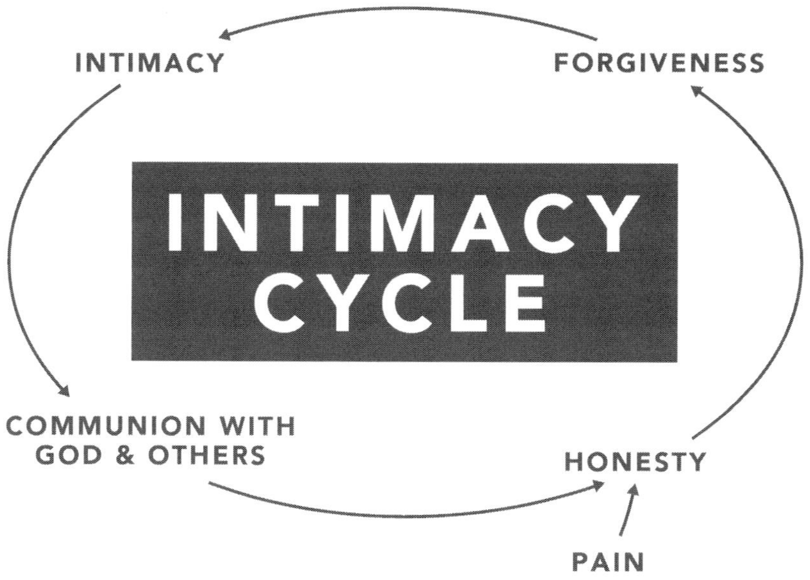

It's easy when facing this choice—whether or not to tell the truth—to worry about what will happen when the truth comes out. What if you're honest and those close to you won't forgive you? It's important to remember that forgiveness and healing take time, and your disclosure may only be the beginning of a long and winding journey toward wholeness. Those you've hurt with your addictions may need time to process—all you can do is be honest and trust God to do His part.

Telling the truth is the first step back into community, both with God and those around you.[51]

But what is it about community that's so important?

We all can sense it. We felt it when we were kids at school and it was reinforced as we grew older. Even now, whether we have it or not, we recognize it to be true.

Being part of a community is important. Johann Hari makes an excellent point: "The opposite of addiction is not sobriety. The opposite of addiction is connection."[52] And Genesis 2:18 says, "It is not good for the man to be alone. I will make a helper suitable for him."

In an article from Rogers Behavioral Health, Deanna Kolas lists out the benefits of belonging to a community.

Community can reverse patterns associated with mental health struggles.[53] We see and experience the downward spiral that occurs when we don't have the community we need. We feel down, even depressed, and this leads to a desire to withdraw from

[51] Nick Stumbo, *Setting Us Free: An Unexpected Journey of Grace* (Gresham: Pure Desire Ministries International, 2015).

[52] Johann Hari, "Everything you think you know about addiction is wrong," TED Talk, June 2015, **https://www.ted.com/talks/johann_hari_everything_you_think_you_know_about_addiction_is_wrong**.

[53] Deanna Kolas, "Community: 5 benefits and how to find yours," *Rogers Behavioral Health*, August 12, 2023, **https://rogersbh.org/blog/community-5-benefits-and-how-find-yours/**.

the community, which in turn causes our symptoms of loneliness and depression to grow worse. We become more isolated. And on it goes, as described in the Shame Cycle earlier in this chapter.

But entering into a community of people can actually reverse the cycle, help us face shame, and bring us up out of our lonely depths. Community has a way of pressing pause on the loneliness and mental health struggles. It can even help us begin to address our addictions.

Communities help people feel less alone. According to an advisory released by the surgeon general in 2023, the United States is facing an epidemic of loneliness, and those who do not have connections within a community experience an increased risk of death that is comparable to the risks of smoking 15 cigarettes a day.[54] But being in a community can help alleviate our sense of loneliness. Regular interaction, sharing ideas, supporting one another, and offering encouragement all contribute to someone feeling less alone. These things can only happen while living in community.

Often, when it comes to compulsive sexual behaviors, it's our loneliness that makes us feel like we're the only ones, and that we will never be able to make any meaningful change. Community fights these feelings of helplessness and hopelessness.

54 Juana Summers, Vincent Acovino, and Christopher Intagliata, "America has a loneliness epidemic. Here are 6 steps to address it," NPR, May 2, 2023, **https://www.npr.org/2023/05/02/1173418268/loneliness-connection-mental-health-dementia-surgeon-general**.

Belonging to a community can help shift unhelpful beliefs about oneself and provide a sense of purpose. "Many people struggling with mental health may also experience a sense of low self-worth. Engaging with community and fostering relationships can help people shift those unhelpful beliefs and learn healthier patterns of relating to themselves and others."[55]

Compulsive sexual behaviors and addictions can pound away at someone's self-worth. Being in a community, and especially a healthy Christian community, can help illustrate God's love and remind someone that they are valuable outside of their sexuality.

Communities increase a person's ability to receive support. Imagine someone at home, alone and addicted to pornography. How will they receive support? Who can they go to in order to receive help? What could come into their lives that would help them change their compulsive behaviors?

According to the Barna report, 48% said no one knows about their struggle and 82% said no one is helping them … but people who attended a church with a support group for pornography were four times more likely to say that someone was helping them![56]

---

[55] Deanna Kolas, "Community: 5 benefits and how to find yours," *Rogers Behavioral Health*, August 12, 2023, **https://rogersbh.org/blog/community-5-benefits-and-how-find-yours/**.

[56] Pure Desire Ministries, *Beyond the Porn Phenomenon: Equipping the Church for a New Conversation about Pornography, Betrayal Trauma, and Healing* (Ventura: Barna Group, 2024), 6, 13.

This is why community is so valuable for people struggling with compulsive sexual behavior—community becomes the place where growth and change occur. A seed won't grow if it's isolated and on its own, but if it's planted in a garden and receives the other things it needs, it can multiply.

Community is like a garden.

Communities provide for accountability. We can try to change—we can even begin to change—but without community, we have no accountability, and it's all too easy to slip back into old ways of being and doing.

Community, community, community.

Community is actually one of the core values of Pure Desire Ministries because we have seen in thousands of lives that the group experience—true community—is an essential element of healing, growth, and transformation.

And yet, when it comes to our sexuality, most of us have decided to go it alone. Either because of deep shame we hold from previous sexual experiences, or because those around us are communicating that sexuality isn't something to talk about, we remain silent. And in our silence, we remain alone.

Which takes us back to Paul's letter to the Romans 12:3–5:

Because of the privilege and authority God has given me, I give each of you this warning: Don't think you are better than you really are. Be honest in your evaluation of yourselves, measuring yourselves by the faith God has given us. [4] *Just as our bodies have many parts and each part has a special function,* [5] *so it is with Christ's body.* ***We are many parts of one body, and we all belong to each other.***

ROMANS 12:3-5 (NLT, EMPHASIS ADDED)

We are many parts of one body, and we belong to each other.

But what exactly do we mean by the concept of community?

Are we talking about the place where we live, the physical neighborhood? Is that our community? Or when we talk about community, are we referring to the people we see every day? Or is our community the other soccer parents we see on a weekly basis, the folks we sit down beside and chat with for an hour … are they our community? Is it the church we attend two or three weekends per month?

There's a lot of different ways to think about or define your community, but at Pure Desire we've come to the conclusion that true community is built within the structure of a small group of people where you're fully known and fully loved.

True community isn't formed simply by being around people, talking with people, or even spending time with them. Time is an important aspect, but there are plenty of people we spend time with yet never go deep with. Some of the loneliest, most isolated people sit in church every Sunday surrounded by people, yet feel deeply alone in their struggle because no one knows the truth about them.

Where true community takes place, you'll find people who know the nitty-gritty of each other's stories. They know things about each other that at first, they thought no one else would ever know … and yet they still want to spend time with them.

True community equals being fully known and fully loved.

Here's one example of what a true community looks like.

There was a man who was going through the *Seven Pillars of Freedom* material in a Pure Desire small group when he did the exercise of writing down the ten worst moments in his life. He had toiled over that one, trying to decide just how honest to be. At the end of the day, he did it. He wrote down the absolute ten worst things that had ever happened to him, even though they were incredibly personal. He was able to do this because he promised himself he wasn't going to share any of these ten worst experiences.

And while sharing was an option for those in the group, it certainly wasn't required. But after he arrived and heard the others in his group being vulnerable, he decided to go for it. He was going to share his super-personal story—one that was linked to so much shame. Without thinking about it too much, he dove in.

He told them how when he was 12 years old he had a sexual experience with another boy. This part of his childhood story had stuck with him and become so shameful to him. It was something he had barely stopped thinking about all these years, and it was the kind of thing that made him feel like God didn't truly love him anymore. When he finished telling the story, he stopped and looked around, sure that the group was about to reject him. Now that he had told the story, he felt a shiver of nervousness. Maybe he had made a mistake.

But he was in a true community—fully known and fully loved.

One by one, other group members nodded their heads and spoke up.

"That happened to me, too."

"I went through a similar experience."

"You're not the only one."

The shame of this man's experience, something that had clung to him for decades, began melting right off of him. He could sense it there in the room—he wasn't ashamed anymore. The group wasn't justifying or accepting the behavior. They were communicating, instead, that this part of his story did not define him or disqualify him from the community of God's people. He wasn't the only one. And it was by working through the shame of this experience that he began his process of transformation, something that would lead him out of his compulsive sexual behaviors and into true freedom. Not only did he experience freedom from his shame, but also by being brave enough to share, he helped other men feel safe enough to share their stories.

A staff member at Pure Desire talks about how much healing she received from her porn addiction after going through counseling with a certified sex addiction therapist earlier in her life. This was how she was able to find sobriety from her sexual addictions, and it was such an important part of her journey.

But it was nearly two decades later, when she started a Pure Desire group and saw others being transformed, that she was able to break through the shame part of the equation—she had still been feeling ashamed about her porn use even after all those years, even after going through counseling and getting sober. Being part of a community is what set her free.

Counseling can be an important part of our healing journey. But often, because a counselor is paid for their work, it's easy to leave a session and feel like, "Well, they're just saying those things because they're paid to do that. That's their job."

But when we can share our stories in front of our peers, there's a level of freedom that occurs that rarely happens in any other environment.

SEVEN THINGS GROUP TEACHES US

Mike Maxwell wrote a blog for Pure Desire titled, "7 Things Group Taught Me."[57] He has been involved in Pure Desire groups for over eight years, and the things he learned about himself, God, and sexual integrity wouldn't have happened without the valuable experiences and time he spent in those groups.

Here are seven things he learned during that time:

---

[57] Mike Maxwell, "7 Things Group Taught Me," Pure Desire Ministries, October 29, 2020, **https://puredesire.org/blog/7-things-group-taught-me/**.

Humility. During the process of recovery, one thing must be overcome at all costs: Pride. Pride can be incredibly destructive as we journey into this area of sexuality and transformation. Until we can acknowledge God's ways in a spirit of humility and confess those sins, pride will continue to eat away at our lives.

But even confession must be done with a spirit of humility and in the scope of a plan laid out with the help of a trained professional or others who have gone before us in the process. A confession, even one made out of humility—without having a plan in place—can lead to more pain and damage to relationships.

Humility is defined as "a modest or low view of one's own importance; humbleness." Until we can begin to see ourselves and our desires as less important than God's desires, pride will continue to wreak havoc in our lives. Being in a group can help us witness and learn to practice humility.

Having humility also allows us to remember what we're truly up against. In 1 Peter 5:8–9 it says,

> *Be alert and of sober mind. Your enemy the devil prowls around like a roaring lion looking for someone to devour.*
> *9 Resist him, standing firm in the faith, because you know that the family of believers throughout the world is undergoing the same kind of sufferings.*

Pride will devour us, but by embracing humility, we find the path to resistance and a firm faith.

Repentance. The second lesson we have seen play out in the groups has been the importance of true confession … and the somewhat radical nature of it. Jesus uses the example of cutting off our hand or gouging out an eye. While Jesus wasn't telling us to literally maim ourselves, he was illustrating the sometimes drastic nature of true repentance. Actionable repentance is so important for the healing process.

This idea of repentance also builds on the concept of humility—until we humble ourselves, we won't be able to bring ourselves to a place of repentance. And being in a group can help us get there.

Accountability. So often the fight to overcome compulsive sexual behavior is a fight for our spiritual lives as well as for our family and our marriage. It could take up to five years of committed engagement to retrain and renew our minds, and this won't happen without a willingness to submit to the accountability of others. It takes time to build enduring character and integrity, and we need the help of others, especially those who understand what we're going through and are willing to ask us questions that help us self-reflect and challenge ourselves. "As iron sharpens iron, so a friend sharpens a friend" (Proverbs 27:17 NLT).

Being in a group gives us a set of people who want to see us succeed and who will help us through these battles.

God's Word. Being in groups has shown us at Pure Desire just how important Scripture can be in our transformation. If we're going to do the hard work of rewiring our brains, we have to start each and every day with devotional time and memorizing Scripture. Even Jesus fought temptation through the recitation of Scriptures, and this is what helped Him overcome Satan in the wilderness.

When we get together in our groups, we talk about the Scriptures that help us the most, and we are able to encourage each other by using verses from the Bible. In a group, we can also witness that God's promises in Scripture are true, and that transformation is available to us.

We always recommend that each person finds a passage of Scripture that serves as a personal promise from God to directly combat the specific lies and shame they might be feeling. These verses can serve as reinforcements when tough situations tempt us to return to old patterns and ways of living.

These are a few that have served group members well on their journey:

But you are a chosen people, a royal priesthood, a holy nation, God's special possession, that you may declare the praises of him who called you out of darkness into his wonderful light. Once you were not a people, but now you are the people of God; once you had not received mercy, but now you have received mercy.

1 PETER 2:9–10

Jesus Christ is the same yesterday and today and forever.

HEBREWS 13:8

Keep your lives free from the love of money and be content with what you have, because God has said, "Never will I leave you; never will I forsake you." So we say with confidence, "The Lord is my helper; I will not be afraid. What can mere mortals do to me?"

HEBREWS 13:5–6

No, in all these things we are more than conquerors through him who loved us.

ROMANS 8:37

I know what it is to be in need, and I know what it is to have plenty. I have learned the secret of being content in any and every situation, whether well fed or hungry, whether living in plenty or in want. I can do all this through him who gives me strength.

PHILIPPIANS 4:12–13

When we find ourselves despairing or giving up hope, having a verse to go to—Scripture to meditate on—can make all the difference.

Gratitude. Compulsive sexual behavior is so often about wanting what we don't have, and if we're not careful, we'll always want more, more, more. We need to learn to practice gratitude and be grateful on a daily basis for what God has given us, and in doing so we reject chasing that which we do not have. When we are thankful for those in our lives, it effectively shuts down our insatiable desire for more.

Being in groups can help us be thankful … because often the group becomes one of the things we most appreciate! The people who have come around us can illustrate what it looks like to be truly grateful, and when we see someone with a grateful heart, we want to be more that way ourselves.

Service. At the foundation of sexual addiction and compulsive sexual behaviors lies greed, covetousness, and selfishness. This isn't always where the behaviors begin, but it is often what cements them in place: we can't get enough, we want what others have, and we pursue these things without any thought or concern for others.

"When we sow selfishness by engaging in sexual sin, we become increasingly filled with lust and selfishness, and that continues to blind us to the realities of what we are doing and how it affects those around us."[58] Groups have shown us that if someone is serious about defeating their compulsive sexual behaviors, they have to take their eyes off of themselves and selflessly serve those around them. And often this service begins right there in the group, where we as individuals, fighting many of the same battles, can hold each other up and care for one another.

Seek professional help. If we've seen anything in groups, it's the importance of hiring professionals as a supplement to your group experience, especially those who understand sexual addiction and are certified specifically in this area. Whether it's help in navigating the minefield of confession or in unpacking our childhood sexual experiences, a professional counselor can eliminate many potential complications.

But we also emphasize that meeting with a professional counselor or psychologist isn't enough on its own. Groups have shown us the incredibly crucial nature of not doing this journey on our own.

---

[58] Mike Maxwell, "7 Things Group Taught Me," Pure Desire Ministries, October 29, 2020, **https://puredesire.org/blog/7-things-group-taught-me/**.

COMMUNITY FOR THE BETRAYED SPOUSE

Those who've struggled with compulsive sexual behavior are not the only ones who need community. Spouses who have experienced betrayal also need support.

Before we move into this section, it's important that we all understand the definition of betrayal trauma: "Betrayal trauma occurs when the people or institutions on which a person depends for survival significantly violate that person's trust or well-being."[59] Betrayal trauma has a significant impact on someone's life and relationships—not only with the person or institution that betrayed them, but with every other interaction they have.

When it comes to the use of porn, a sense of betrayal is common.

> *Far from short-term, these damaging emotions and betrayals can linger and take time to heal. Just under half of women who had a partner or spouse who regularly viewed porn (46%) say they have fully recovered from the effects of this (vs. 59% of men who had a partner or spouse who regularly viewed porn). The remainder of these women seem to still be working through this experience in some fashion (21% have somewhat recovered, 12% are somewhat still healing, 13% are still healing and 8% are unsure).*

---

[59] Jennifer J. Freyd, "What Is a Betrayal Trauma? What Is Betrayal Trauma Theory?," University of Oregon, August 23, 2023, **https://dynamic.uoregon.edu/jjf/defineBT.html**.

> *This data underscores a troubling reality: The emotional wounds inflicted by a partner's regular porn use are not only more severe for women but also have a longer-lasting impact.*[60]

Why is this important? There's often a forgotten person when it comes to compulsive sexual behaviors or sexual addictions, and that person is the partner of the one who's struggling. When the struggler comes forward and confesses or finally gets caught, the spotlight is on them—what they need to find freedom, what they need in order to transform. While this is a natural response, it often leaves the betrayed spouse getting overlooked for care or support. Imagine a horrible car accident takes place, but when the paramedics arrive, they only care for the driver and not the others who were hurt!

The betrayed spouse can be overlooked in the chaos of confession or the rush of getting help for the one who is struggling. The betrayed spouse may even *want* to be overlooked, having so many conflicting feelings and perhaps even unsure of how they want to move ahead in life. They may not want the spotlight on them because they are paralyzed with pain, humiliated and fearful, unsure how to move forward, or feel that since it's not their addiction they shouldn't need to find help. Maybe they're trying to figure out what about their marriage was true and what was false.

---

[60] Pure Desire Ministries, *Beyond the Porn Phenomenon: Equipping the Church for a New Conversation about Pornography, Betrayal Trauma, and Healing* (Ventura: Barna Group, 2024), 56.

At the end of the day, sometimes the betrayed spouse is the hardest one to convince of their need for community. I (Ashley) remember being there. I didn't understand how traumatized I was. I was angry at the idea of needing "help" when I didn't do any of this. The problem was my husband's, so I believed if he got help, our problems would end.

But even after he sought help and started making progress in his recovery, I was still stuck in agonizing pain. I knew I couldn't stay in that condition and be a healthy and present mom, so I finally decided to try Pure Desire's *Betrayal & Beyond.* Immediately, when I started reading through the workbook, I felt seen. I was reading words that put language to what I was experiencing, allowing me to "trust the process" even if I didn't fully understand why I needed to do so much work for a problem I didn't create. Many of these thoughts ran through my head:

Why do I need to commit months of my life to going through these meetings when none of this is my fault?

Why do I have to add one more commitment to my already-busy schedule? I didn't do anything wrong.

Why do I need community when this isn't my addiction?

Why can't he just stop without me going to a group and facing potential embarrassment?

I don't want to go to a group—when I'm not even sure I want to stay in this marriage.

These are all common questions and thoughts the betrayed spouse might have; yet community is more important than ever for someone going through what they're going through. Because what a lot of us don't understand is that betrayal trauma is real. When someone we love has been deceitful and/or unfaithful, neglected us, or has put our health or livelihood in danger, it turns our world on its head. It can be hard to make sense of what's going on or find any direction in life. Meanwhile, because the pain is excruciating, we may feel like we can't trust anyone anymore, and the sense that we need to simply hunker down and protect ourselves can paralyze us from doing the things we need to do.

Betrayed spouses may want to run, cry, scream, get revenge, or wake up from the nightmare. They may want so badly to understand, sympathize, or protect. There are so many different responses, and none of them are wrong. Here are just a few of the possible responses to betrayal you might experience:[61]

- Intrusive thoughts and images
- Nightmares or flashbacks
- Avoidance of behaviors
- Hypervigilance
- Irritability or angry outbursts

We'll introduce and discuss a more comprehensive list later, but just know that you could experience a wide variety of emotions and physical responses.

What's important to remember is that, in the same way someone would seek treatment if they were in a serious accident caused by another person, betrayed spouses need to seek treatment

[61] MindWell Psychology NYC, "Top Betrayal Trauma Signs, Triggers & Strategies to Recovery," October 12, 2021, **https://mindwellnyc.com/top-betrayal-trauma-signs-triggers-strategies-to-recovery-2022/**.

for the trauma they've experienced. It may not have been their fault, but it did happen to them, and now it's time to take care of themselves.

A huge part of this treatment is entering into a community of others who have gone through a similar experience—people who can help them begin to unpack their pain and find a new way forward.

Joining a group helped me (Ashley) become more aware of what I was feeling, thinking, and how my body was responding to betrayal, while also giving me the tools I needed in order to process my experiences. Instead of being worn out, sick, and emotionally unhealthy, being in a group helped me to keep my mind and body as healthy as possible.

The transformation isn't just external or physical—it is also emotional and psychological. For example, I realized that my outbursts directed at my kids lessened when I was consistently working through my Pure Desire group for betrayed spouses. All of my bottled-up hurt and anger were being taken care of in a way that didn't harm the people around me. A deep peace began to settle inside of me.

Was I still hurt? Of course! Did I still occasionally feel angry, sad, betrayed, and all of the other feelings? Yes! But everything inside me was on an upward, healing trajectory. Being part of the community was transforming me.

Joining a group can also be so valuable for a betrayed spouse because it gives an opportunity to walk with others who have experienced many of the same experiences and emotions. Proverbs 19:20 (NLT) says, "Get all the advice and instruction you can, so you will be wise the rest of your life." This is what happens in a community setting: we receive wise counsel and can begin to see our situation from the outside, giving us much-needed perspective and insight. In that group, when you receive wisdom or hear what others are going through, it is incredibly empowering.

Finally, when a betrayed spouse is in a group, it gives them permission to feel whatever it is that they're feeling. Often, betrayed spouses turn the blame on themselves:

If only I was more sexual.

If only I hadn't gained weight.

If only I didn't voice my opinions and stir up trouble.

If only I created a more welcoming home.

If only I took on more of the parenting responsibilities so he wouldn't be so stressed.

If only I didn't have to travel out of town.

Sometimes when a betrayed spouse talks to close friends after the betrayal comes out, their friends will tell them they shouldn't feel that way, that it's not their fault, that they don't have to carry that burden, and more. But in the community of a group, betrayed spouses are given the freedom to feel whatever it is that they're feeling. They can be great one day and hopeless the next. They can be encouraged one day and completely discouraged the next. But even if they're feeling this roller coaster of emotions, the group will reassure them that what they're feeling is normal. They won't be stuck there forever.

For me (Nick), my wife felt similar to Ashley, wondering, "Why do I have to go through this? This isn't my problem!" It wasn't until she joined a Betrayal & Beyond group that my wife realized the burden she had been carrying. My secrets had become her secrets—no one around us knew the truth, because I was their pastor, friend, or family member. When my wife was able to open up and process with other women who could relate to her journey, she finally felt seen and heard. This became an incredibly healing environment for her.

Having the right tools and relationships, along with a process you can trust, gives the betrayed spouse something to fall back on when life simply feels too difficult.

The fallout of addiction and compulsive sexual behaviors impacts everyone close by.

Joining a group and finding community is one of the best steps you can take toward transformation and healing.

While finding community is an important part of the betrayed spouse's healing, there are also things the struggling spouse can do in order to help the process along.

First, the struggling spouse can apologize that their choices have caused their spouse pain. Sometimes the struggler assumes their spouse knows they are sorry; after all, they're acting contrite, they're seeking help for their compulsive behaviors, and they're doing their best to make amends. This is all important, but the words, "I'm sorry I caused you pain," hearing those words spoken out loud, can actually be an important step in the healing process for the betrayed spouse.

Second, the struggling spouse can acknowledge that their prior choices have led to a situation where the betrayed spouse has to take time and emotional energy to find healing. It's a difficult process for the betrayed spouse to undertake, and it can be a long journey that in many ways distracts them from their family, their job, and other things they love. When the struggling spouse recognizes the pain and sacrifice of the betrayed spouse, it can be deeply meaningful and validating for them.

It's important for the struggling spouse to be proactive in offering to care for the children or other responsibilities so that the betrayed spouse can attend their group. Managing a home, kids, a career, and more is already a lot to carry. Finding the time to attend a support group can feel overwhelming for a betrayed spouse. If the struggler offers to fill this need, not only is it helpful, but it might also be what's practically required in order for the betrayed spouse to have the margin to be able to get the help they need.

What's crucial in recovery, for the one who has struggled as well as for the betrayed spouse, is breaking the chains of isolation. When we talk about joining a community, a true community where you are fully known and fully loved, what we're really talking about is having the courage to move out of the shadows of isolation and into the light.

But moving out of isolation can be one of the most significant hurdles there is in recovery. Isolation isn't just about being alone—it's a pattern that gets created around withdrawing and avoiding meaningful relationships, often stemming from a desire to avoid difficult situations, conversations, or internal confrontations with what's really going on in our lives.

Negative habits grow in the darkness of isolation, like a fungus that flourishes in the dark. Continuing in isolation only serves to feed the shame and prevent us from all the gifts of community we've been talking about. This journey out of isolation and into community is our first step toward healing and freedom, and it's when we embrace community that we find the strength to engage in healthier behaviors, with ourselves and others. God has made us to "never walk alone."

We, especially as Christians, are called to live our lives within the boundaries and blessings of community.

Carry each other's burdens, and in this way you will fulfill the law of Christ.

GALATIANS 6:2

Therefore confess your sins to each other and pray for each other so that you may be healed.

JAMES 5:16

And though a man might prevail against one who is alone, two will withstand him—a threefold cord is not quickly broken.

ECCLESIASTES 4:12 (ESV)

"For where two or three gather in my name,
there am I with them."

MATTHEW 18:20

Those last words are Jesus' words to His disciples. When we gather with a community, when we come together and tell the truth, showing each other God's love, we create with God an incredible capacity for transformation.

And it's in these transformative spaces that true healing can be experienced.

PART THREE

HEALING

CHAPTER EIGHT

HEALING FOR THE INDIVIDUAL

Remember the story we told in Chapter One about the young man named Kurt who had been exposed to porn early in his life? Remember how he couldn't quit … or, rather, how he quit time and time again but it never stuck?

One of the common concerns for those who want to quit but are afraid to address the problem is how their spouse will respond. Will they get angry? Will they be hurt?

Will they leave?

Kurt was one of the many who've come forward despite these concerns—he knew that if he was going to make any kind of meaningful change, it had to start with complete honesty and openness. First, he talked to a counselor about the best way to disclose to his wife the secrets he'd been keeping all those years. Next, with a written game plan in hand, he told her, and while it wasn't easy, and while she felt hurt and betrayed, it felt like he was finally making meaningful progress and owning his choices. Finally, he and his wife both joined Pure Desire groups, and this gave them the time, space, and tools they both needed to set out on a journey of true healing. The process took time, and they had some difficult trust issues to work through, but now they would both say their marriage is stronger than it has ever been.

Rather than being built on a false foundation of half-truth, they are building a new, deeper connection that is rooted in honesty, humility, and trust.

So what are some of the keys when it comes to discovering this deep transformation? How can the individual change their patterns and their brain's way of operating in order to find freedom from their addiction?

Earlier in the book we talked about how resilient and malleable the human brain is, how it can heal and grow long after we're children. Our brains are capable of great change. We can train them to relinquish old connections and form new, even stronger ones.

Another way of thinking about this is mental toughness, and this mental toughness is extremely important on an individual's road to healing from compulsive sexual behaviors and sex addictions. So, how can we develop mental toughness? How can we develop a mindset for healing that will help us in the process of renewing our minds?

Do not conform to the pattern of this world, but be transformed by the renewing of your mind. Then you will be able to test and approve what God's will is—his good, pleasing and perfect will.

ROMANS 12:2

That's what mental toughness is all about—transforming and renewing our minds so that we can walk in the perfect will God has for us.

So where do we begin?

Here is how Pure Desire's neuroscience expert, Heather Kolb, explains the process of creating mental toughness.[62] The model for mental toughness that we're going to walk through isn't just a grin-and-bear-it kind of process. It's not just us saying: try harder, and then you try harder. These are concrete steps you can take to improve your mental toughness.

And this isn't just something we use at Pure Desire—it's actually a model that's used in many different environments.

In fact, one environment where they've tested and developed these tools is in the Navy SEALs, in what they call their Pool Competency Test. In this test, they are training their recruits to survive underwater, a place that's completely adverse to human survival. Being underwater, with the constant threat of drowning, is one of the toughest environments you can enter.

This is how it goes: the trainers have their recruits go underwater with their scuba tanks, and then the trainers intentionally sabotage them. They disconnect their hoses, strike them, pull off their face masks, and basically put them in a situation where their life is on the line.

Now, prior to implementing the mental toughness tools we're going to talk about, less than 25% of Navy SEAL recruits were

[62] The information in this chapter comes from our course, *Sexual Integrity 101*, presented by Heather Kolb. She's a professor, a mom, a wife, and an expert on neuroscience, and she has spent 20 years studying human behavior. In this particular session of the course, she walks us through the process of developing mental toughness and other practical tools for renewing the mind.

able to pass the pool competency test. But after implementing these practices and ways of thinking, the pass-rate went up to 33%.[63]

The first practice is goal-setting. We hear about goal-setting frequently in our culture, so this might initially feel somewhat trite or cliché. The truth is, however, that appropriate goal-setting helps us move in the direction of our preferred future. When we clearly define where we are headed—and the steps needed to get there—we can begin to make powerful changes!

Now, within goal-setting there are three basic rules you want to keep in mind.

The first one is to set no more than three goals for yourself at a time. Sometimes, especially when we want to change, when we're excited about change and feeling optimistic, we might write down ten or twelve things we want to change about ourselves or achieve or accomplish.

The problem is, as the days pass and the list is sitting there staring us in the face, we get easily overwhelmed, realize we were doomed from the beginning, and throw the list straight into the trash. We're right back where we started, reverting to all our old coping behaviors and old ways of living.

So, it's important to write down no more than three goals at a time (at the most), and as we accomplish each of those goals, we get a healthy rush of dopamine, a sense of accomplishment, and

---

[63] Bakari Akil, "How the Navy Seals Increased Passing Rates: Better passing rates through simple psychology." *Psychology Today*, November 9, 2009, **https://www.psychologytoday.com/us/blog/communication-central/200911/how-the-navy-seals-increased-passing-rates**.

then, as we cross that item off our list, we can add a new goal at the bottom.

The second rule with goal-setting is to focus on short-term goals. Often, folks in this environment of recovery can struggle with depressive behaviors and find long-term goals overwhelming and impossible. Short-term goals can be helpful—things like, "I'm going to make it to my group today," or, "Today, I'm going to get out of my pajamas." These kinds of short-term goals can be so helpful in reversing old mindsets and creating a sense of positivity and forward-thinking.

The third rule of goal-setting is to set positive goals. Again, in this environment of recovery, it's easy for all of our goals to be negative: don't watch porn, don't fantasize, don't look at these certain things. We tend to focus on the things we don't want to do instead of really learning and focusing on what we want to do.

One example would be, instead of making a goal of not binge-watching a television show, make your goal to go on a walk for twenty minutes. If we can set positive goals for ourselves, often the negative behaviors fade, lost in the positive environment we're creating for ourselves.

So, never set more than three goals for yourself; focus on short-term goals; and set positive goals.

The second practice that helps us develop mental toughness is mental rehearsal.

The SEALs hired psychologists to come into the program and work with the recruits on the pool competency exam, along with other areas of their development. What they found was that the recruits who practiced mental rehearsal, or visualization, were far more successful. So, for example, recruits fared much better in the underwater test if they beforehand envisioned themselves being attacked under water. Then they thought through what actions they would take, as well as envisioned what it looked like to get through that tough experience successfully. When they went through it in their mind, they developed mental toughness that carried through into the moment.

So, what part of your recovery seems the toughest to you? Which part feels impossible, or is something you've tried to do in the past but haven't been able to achieve?

What we need to do is take this difficult thing and envision doing it. Mentally rehearse going through the challenge successfully.

Do you know why this works? Your brain, as smart as it is, doesn't differentiate between *imagining* yourself going through this challenge and *actually* going through the challenge. In your brain, it's all the same. This is why the Bible has so much to say about **meditation**. Meditation is a way of imagining the world, and our lives, as God sees them. When we rehearse this truth, it begins to alter the way we think!

For some of us, going to group each week is a huge challenge. There are plenty of reasons many of us would simply rather not go. But mental rehearsal can be incredibly helpful in actually getting us to attend these all-important meetings.

Maybe your mental rehearsal could look like this:

You envision yourself getting ready to go and then going out and climbing in your car. You put on certain music or listen to a particular podcast. You stop and get coffee on your way, and then you envision making the drive to your group meeting. Once there, you park the car, walk inside, and enter the space where your group meets.

Envisioning this ahead of time, and re-envisioning it multiple times, can be so helpful because then when the time comes to actually go to group, your brain will think, *Okay, I've done this before. This is doable.* When you mentally rehearse difficult things, you are helping to wire together the neurons and neural pathways that are required for you to get to your meeting.

There's another aspect of mental rehearsal that's important, and it's developing an attitude of gratitude. This is something that's been studied extensively in the field of psychology, and what they're suggesting now is that gratitude is a personality characteristic that can be developed. It means having a distinct awareness of the goodness in your life. Scripture also repeats this truth—*I will enter his courts with thanksgiving in my heart; I will enter his courts with praise* (Psalm 100:4, paraphrase). Gratitude has a way of bringing us more fully into the presence of God and His goodness around us.

Individuals who exhibit and express more gratitude are happier, healthier and more energetic. They are less likely to experience physical ailments like headaches, stomachaches, and nausea, and they're less likely to feel lonely, stressed, or depressed.[64] For many of us, when life is going great, it's so easy to have gratitude and feel thankful for the good things in our lives, but when life takes a turn for the worse, suddenly gratitude doesn't come so naturally.

At Pure Desire, we've recognized and implemented gratitude into our curriculum—in most of the journaling that we encourage people to do, we ask them to write out the things that they're thankful for. Even that simple act of writing about the good in our lives, even when we're not feeling good, gives us the opportunity to start retraining our brain, creating new neural pathways, and then allowing our feelings to catch up with the reality of our lives.

Mentally rehearse the things you want to do in your life but perhaps currently find challenging. Pair that with deliberate gratitude for the good in your life. This will take you a long way in creating mental toughness.

The third practice that will help you gain mental toughness is positive self-talk. Before you dismiss this as some kind of minor, "self-help" tool, consider this: Did you know that we talk to ourselves at the rate of 300 to 1,000 words a minute? That's at least four times faster than we can talk out loud! That's a lot of talking.

---

[64] Ellen G. Goldman, "The Power of Gratitude," *SparkPeople*, August 24, 2010, **https://www.sparkpeople.com/resource/wellness_articles.asp?id=1541**.

Think about that for a moment—if we wake up in a bad mood, it would only take about five minutes to speak 4,000 negative words to ourselves. In five minutes, we can set the tone for our day by tearing down and discouraging ourselves … before we're even barely awake. It doesn't take long for the voice in our heads to spiral into negativity.

When I (Nick) was in the midst of my struggle with pornography, I felt totally worthless. And it wasn't simply something I felt at an abstract level—I believed it, too. I believed that because of this addiction I had, my value as a person was less, and no matter how many people tried to encourage me or say positive things, those compliments just rolled right off my back. They didn't stick. I simply couldn't believe them because nobody knew what was happening at a deeper, secretive level. But I did. This made the negative, accusing self-talk much louder than any encouragement from others.

It was almost as if everything in my life was filtered through the lens of my struggle with pornography. So if I read somewhere that Jesus loved me, that I'm a child of God, perhaps a verse like 1 John 3:1 …

> *See what great love the Father has lavished on us, that we should be called children of God! And that is what we are!*

… I couldn't accept it or experience it because all I saw was what I was doing. Sure, the Bible said the Father loves us so much that He's made us His children, but in my heart I didn't believe it was talking about me. I had trouble separating who I was from what I was doing, and because I was doing things I was ashamed of, I felt rotten to the core.

Maybe you have trouble with negative self-talk. Maybe you've done things in the past you're ashamed of, or maybe you have a habit, an unwanted behavior, or an addiction that you keep beating yourself up about.

Stop for a minute and ask yourself a question:

Where are those negative messages coming from?

It's important to try to figure out where and why these negative messages are gaining energy in our lives. Are we surrounding ourselves with people who are also speaking negatively—either about us or themselves? Have we internalized negative messages about ourselves through the years? Start examining (perhaps with a counselor) where your negative self-talk originates.

Secondly, it's impossible to stop thinking about something simply by telling ourselves to stop thinking about it. Then you're thinking about it! If you tell yourself not to think of a giraffe, what do you think of? A giraffe. You won't stop negative self-talk simply by telling yourself to stop doing it.

We have to replace those negative thoughts with something positive. For so many of us, these are the lies that the enemy wants us to believe about ourselves, the lies that will keep us in isolation and far away from an environment of healing.

Remember all the brain talk from earlier in the book? Our limbic system is where this self-talk lives, and it's fully developed by the time we're 6 years old, but our prefrontal cortex, the more rational part of our brain, isn't fully developed until we're 25.[65] So we spend nearly twenty years with this fully functional, highly emotional part of our brain, and it becomes the filter. Any lies we form during this time become effectively internalized.

If we want to create a new positive pathway—new ideas of positive self-talk—we have to be intentional.

Remember how neurons that fire together wire together?

Well, here's another one for you.

Neurons out of sync fail to link.[66]

What we mean by this is that the more we stop our unhealthy behaviors, replacing them with new behaviors, the old neurological pathways break apart. And over time, they don't have the power over us that they did at one time.

Every day, we're waking up with brand new baby neurons that are just waiting to be used for something amazing!

This is one reason we need to be in a group, why we need a healthy community: when we speak our negative self-talk out loud in a community of committed and loving people, they can help us recognize how untrue and damaging it is. We need other people in our lives who will speak truth into our lives and give us the words to transform our negative self-talk into positive self-talk.

---

[65] Arain M, Haque M, Johal L, et al. "Maturation of the adolescent brain." *Neuropsychiatr Dis Treat*. 2013;9:449-461. doi:10.2147/NDT.S39776.

[66] Nathan Collins, "Pathways from the Eye to the Brain," *Stanford Medicine Magazine*, August 21, 2017, **https://stanmed.stanford.edu/carla-shatz-vision-brain/**.

The fourth and final practice that will help you gain mental toughness is something called arousal control. At Pure Desire, we often refer to arousal as "going limbic," meaning our thinking brain—our prefrontal cortex—starts to shut off, while our reactive, survival brain—our limbic system—takes over. When we begin to feel stressed, our brain switches to a completely different way of operating. And arousal in these instances can take many forms—it can be sexual, yes, but it can also be the arousal of our appetite or of an emotion. Whatever form arousal takes, it becomes important to be able to calm our brain in stressful situations, to calm our limbic system, to reengage our prefrontal cortex, and bring our entire body back into a calm state of being.

This isn't only helpful in gaining mental toughness—it's also crucial in our journey toward healing.

So, where do we begin?

There's actually a very simple breathing exercise that helps calm the limbic system and reengage the prefrontal cortex, and it's called the four by four.[67] We're going to breathe in to the count of four, pause, and then breathe out to the count of four.

Some may think you've been breathing your entire life, not to mention all day, so how can breathing in a certain way be that important?

[67] Cleveland Clinic, "How Box Breathing Can Help You Destress," August 17, 2021, **https://health.clevelandclinic.org/box-breathing-benefits**.

Give it a try.

Sit comfortably in a chair, close your eyes, and begin breathing. Four seconds in, pause, four seconds out. Intentionally slow down and keep to the rhythm. Allow your shoulders to drop, and when you breathe, take deep breaths from your diaphragm.

Breathe in, pause, breathe out.

Something that adds another level to this breathing exercise is incorporating a Scripture verse that you repeat in your mind as you breathe—this pairs the physical and mental benefits of measured breathing along with the spiritual and emotional benefits of repeating Scripture and positive self-talk.

One example goes like this, using Philippians 4:13:

(breathe in for four seconds) "I can do all things"

(pause) "through Christ"

(breathe out for four seconds) "who strengthens me."

(breathe in for four seconds) "I can do all things"

(pause) "through Christ"

(breathe out for four seconds) "who strengthens me."

(breathe in for four seconds) "I can do all things"

(pause) "through Christ"

(breathe out for four seconds) "who strengthens me."

This is one of the most healing things you can do in your day. Scientists have studied this idea of breathing and meditation and have found that when we're going about our day, our neurons are firing in all different directions, managing all kinds of thoughts and feelings and emotions and actions. But when we take time to breathe and meditate, our neurons actually start to fire in synchrony.[68]

If we can do this three times a day for just a few minutes, it will do amazing things in the process of renewing the mind and increasing our mental toughness. Several Psalms tell us how David meditated on God's law day and night—it is constantly on his lips. David was practicing arousal control long before we called it that. Rather than focusing his mind on the problems and threats around him, he continually brought his heart and mind back to God's truth. We may not be David, but we can do this as well!

One last but very important thing about arousal control has to do with the technological age in which we live. Research is showing a strong correlation between internet use (including social media) and addictive behaviors. Research suggests that "social media interferes with clear thinking and decision making, causing a lack of self-control and impulsive behaviors."[69] Now,

---

[68] Lisa Brunette, "Richard Davidson's research cited: the effect of meditation on brain," University of Wisconsin-Madison, Waisman Center, November 16, 2004, **https://www.waisman.wisc.edu/2004/11/16/richard-davidsons-research-cited-the-effect-of-meditation-on-brain/**.

[69] Keith Wilcox, Andrew T. Stephen, "Are Close Friends the Enemy? Online Social Networks, Self-Esteem, and Self-Control," *Journal of Consumer Research*, Volume 40, Issue 1, 1 June 2013, Pages 90–103, **https://doi.org/10.1086/668794**.

we're not saying that the internet is evil—it's not. But we have to figure out how to have healthy online behaviors, because the same study suggests that "greater social media use is associated with a higher body mass index, increased binge eating, a lower credit score, and higher levels of credit card debt."

When it comes to renewing our mind, what does it look like for us to have healthy internet use plans? What does renewing our minds look like on a daily basis?

It all starts when we wake up in the morning—we need to begin our day by meditating on the Lord and on His Word. This might mean keeping important Scripture verses next to our bed, something that we see first thing in the morning. Maybe it means expressing our thanks to God for our blessings when we're in the shower—not just quietly, but out loud, so that we're hearing them. Throughout our day we focus on our short-term goals, mentally rehearsing what the rest of our day is going to look like and what we'll choose to do that evening. And then a half hour before we go to sleep, we're going to unplug from all our screens so we can put our brains in the right state of mind to get some rest.

Because even when we have our phones in our rooms with us at night, we're conditioned to respond to any sound or light it emits. One of the best things you can do to eliminate compulsive behaviors in your life is to keep your cell phone out of your bedroom.

Imagine that your sexual thought life is a house.[70]

It's late in the evening, you're lying down, maybe your spouse has gone to bed, and you hear that familiar knock of lust.

What are you going to do?

Most people try to create a force field around their house: the internet monitoring, a friend to call for backup, certain sites blocked on their phone. They create a sense of security through the barriers they try to put up between themselves and sin.

In other words, they avoid dealing with the trigger—their thought life. They may put up some good boundaries, but as long as they haven't dealt with their thought life, at some point the barriers will fail, and they'll give in to old ways of thinking and living.

Of course, the opposite of that is just leaving the house wide open, letting your thought life go wherever it wants to go. We don't recommend that either.

What I invite you to do is imagine going out onto the front porch of this house of your thought life, and the next time lust approaches, sit down with it and start a conversation. Ask: at what point in my life did this fantasy appeal to me? Why did porn become appealing to me and at what point in my life?

If we can begin to ask these kinds of questions, we will learn amazing things about ourselves and why we're addicted to

---

[70] Pure Desire Ministries, *Sexual Integrity 101*, Session 4, August 2020. This explanation is presented by guest expert, Jay Stringer: therapist, minister, and award-winning author of *Unwanted: How Sexual Brokenness Reveals Our Way to Healing*.

these things. It's an approach that works for all of our unwanted behaviors or underlying pain. If your back hurts, you could go years treating it with a good gin and tonic or perhaps living on Ibuprofen … or you could ask your back, "What are you communicating to me? When did it become this way?" And maybe you'd remember that nine months ago you were in a car accident and never went to a doctor because it didn't seem that serious.

The same is true of our lust and the neural pathways that have formed to accommodate it. Unaddressed trauma, unaddressed pain, unaddressed anger or anxiety in our lives can be outsourced to porn or other things that won't lead to true healing.

We all need healing. It's okay to make mistakes—that's part of our human condition—but let's put those mistakes on the table and ask, "Is there a better way?"

Let's look at those things in our lives and learn from them.

Though healing from compulsive sexual behavior can be challenging, we have watched thousands of men and women utilize the practices described in this chapter who are now walking in true, lasting transformation.

CHAPTER NINE
HEALING FOR THE BETRAYED SPOUSE

What's been amazing for me (Ashley) has been experiencing healing myself. It's easy to understand why a betrayed spouse would believe the addict is the only one who will experience change and growth after being in a group. What I wasn't expecting was the radical post-traumatic growth I experienced after doing the hard work of healing from betrayal trauma. The National Institutes of Health describes post-traumatic growth as,

> *'... positive psychological changes experienced as a result of the struggle with trauma or highly challenging situations.' This phenomenon should be considered not as an alternative, but as a parallel process with respect to negative psychological consequences. Post-traumatic growth may feature positive changes in self-perception, interpersonal relationships and philosophy of life, leading to increased self-awareness and self-confidence, a more*

open attitude toward others, a greater appreciation of life and the discovery of new possibilities.[71]

I (Ashley) didn't know what to do when I discovered that my husband was addicted to porn, but God led us to Pure Desire, and we both poured ourselves into the material. I began to see, for the first time, that my husband's choices were not my fault but they *were* impacting me emotionally, physically, mentally, sexually, and spiritually. I had trouble controlling my heart rate, breathing, runaway thoughts, anger, and so many more challenges because of the pain and shock. The betrayal I was experiencing was real and it was going to take a lot of time, support, and processing to heal from those wounds. I realized that even Christians weren't perfect, and that sometimes others will do things out of their own pain that hurt you.

It took some time to rewire the parts of my brain that believed I wasn't enough and that my worth was dependent on my husband. I came to recognize how precious I am to God, and as time passed, I learned to identify my feelings, set boundaries to keep myself safe and sane, and explore where and why I stopped believing that I am who God says I am and that He is my source of comfort. As my thinking was transformed, God began to use those dark places—the very things I swore I'd never talk about—to help me find freedom.

---

[71] Dell'Osso L, Lorenzi P, Nardi B, Carmassi C, Carpita B. "Post Traumatic Growth (PTG) in the Frame of Traumatic Experiences," *Clin Neuropsychiatry*. 2022;19(6):390-393. doi:10.36131/cnfioritieditore20220606.

The joy my husband and I feel when we share our story is unmatched, and I want to do everything in my power to stop the madness, break generational curses, and help others experience the same transformation in their minds and their lives.

But almost every single time, in order to find freedom, we have to be able to admit that we have a problem. And often the problem we have isn't simply a behavior that has to be changed but a way of thinking and living that has to be transformed. For many people, it's this past pain that's driving our current behavior—that was the case for me—and until we deal with that pain, it's going to be extremely difficult, nearly impossible, to break the chain of addiction and compulsive sexual behavior.

We can change the way we respond.

With Jesus' help and the support of others, we can change the way our brains function.

There is hope.

I realized that by attending a group it gave me a way to deal with life. I learned how to manage the difficult things that came up, whether it was my husband relapsing or a family tragedy or having a tough week with one of the kids. These are actually tools I didn't learn or have a good example, growing up. Betrayal is never wanted. Trials are never hoped for, but if we choose to lean into the pain and we are willing to learn from it, incredible things can happen and not a drop of that pain will be wasted.

Consider it pure joy, my brothers and sisters, whenever you face trials of many kinds, because you know that the testing of your faith produces perseverance. Let perseverance finish its work so that you may be mature and complete, not lacking anything.

JAMES 1:2–4

It's hard to comprehend until you are on the other side of it. We have heard this testimony thousands of times at Pure Desire.

We can't predict or control what will happen. If our spouse has a relapse with porn, is that the breaking point for the relationship? Or will we work together to address it? Everyone has to answer these questions for themselves, and engaging with a group gives us the support we need.

I was seeing tangible changes in my life. When I was hurting or struggling, the group taught me to reach for the phone and call a group member instead of isolating or coping in self-destructive ways. I began doing solo projects around the house when Jon was out of town rather than worrying and being consumed with fear, and I built some pretty impressive tables and benches in that season! In fact, I distinctly remember Jon going on a work trip for two weeks, and after he returned I realized I hadn't thought about his addiction one single time! That was a huge milestone for me and gave me hope that I didn't have to be chained to his choices or let fear and anxiety rule my life.

Not only was our relationship changing, but my parenting was changing too. I struggled with anger due to growing up without examples of how to properly process thoughts and feelings combined with stuffed trauma. I hated that my anger would come out sideways and land on my kids, and whenever that happened it heaped more shame on me and made me feel like a failed wife and mother.

But as my betrayal trauma started to heal, my anger began to dissipate. My kids were no longer a trigger for me, and I learned how to properly address uncomfortable thoughts and feelings immediately, in the right way. I discovered I wasn't angry with my kids! It was the rest of life seeping into that relationship, and once those other areas of my life began to heal, so did the anger I had been feeling.

Not only that, but I no longer felt this pressure and anxiety to raise perfect kids. I learned the best thing I could do for them was to show them what genuine and unconditional love looked like instead of coming down hard on them when they didn't obey my list of rules.

Finally, my relationship with my mom began to heal. I remember one day she picked me up to go out for breakfast, and I knew she was going to say something about my big curly hair. It was new for me to embrace my natural black girl hair as part of my journey to be confident in who God created me to be. And it happened. She made a remark that hurt me.

Instead of me going silent or exploding (silence or violence), I collected my thoughts and said, "Mom, I'm really trying to embrace who God created me to be. I want to be proud of who I am. Please don't make comments about my hair or my looks—it hurts my feelings. If you're going to make comments today, I'd rather not go to breakfast."

My mom looked at me in shock and said, "Well, aren't you healthy?"

I told her about the work I had been doing and the Pure Desire groups I was leading.

She got very quiet, then said, "Maybe I need one of those groups."

I couldn't believe it! Decades of our toxic cycle started to break right in that car. I helped her get into a group, and about a year later we used one of the tools in both of our resources to help us navigate a cyclical conversation (argument) we had been having my entire adult life. We took turns sharing and making commitments to each other.

When I reflect on our relationship today, I can't believe we used to have such an unhealthy dynamic, and we thought it was normal because we didn't know any better. But this is what happens when you commit to healing—the transformation spreads outward from your relationship with your spouse to your relationships with children, friends, parents, and coworkers. It's completely normal to initially feel hesitant to work on your healing as a betrayed spouse, but as I, and so many others in your shoes can attest, the growth waiting for you is completely worth it!

But it's not easy because betrayal trauma activates a core part of our brain: when we experience a trauma like betrayal, our fight, flight, or freeze response gets activated.[72] This is something our bodies have at their disposal, and it's meant to be short-term and adaptive, which makes sense: when your body goes into that mode, your normal immune function is temporarily shut down. Think about this fight-or-flight response in the case of a tiger chasing you: your body immediately devotes all of its energy and resources to helping you to run fast. It's not thinking about digesting the last thing you ate or sending immune cells to kill a cold virus.

But this is the problem with trauma—it can introduce your body to a prolonged state of fight-or-flight, rendering your body nearly helpless in fighting off sickness. You can enter a state that begins a chronic cascading of inflammatory responses. Your body, embedded in trauma, isn't concerned with long-term health and wellness—it is in survival mode, a mode that can be incredibly damaging to many of your normal bodily functions and responses.

Maybe you're wondering if you're experiencing betrayal trauma. Here's a short list of potential symptoms that might indicate this is what you're dealing with:[73]

- Insomnia
- Fearfulness

[72] Olivia Guy-Evans, "Fight, Flight, Freeze, or Fawn: How We Respond to Threats," *Simply Psychology*, **https://www.simplypsychology.org/fight-flight-freeze-fawn.html**.

[73] MindWell Psychology NYC, "Top Betrayal Trauma Signs, Triggers & Strategies to Recovery," October 12, 2021, **https://mindwellnyc.com/top-betrayal-trauma-signs-triggers-strategies-to-recovery-2022/**.

- Social withdrawal
- Feeling emotionally numb
- Physical symptoms of tension headaches, migraines, and fatigue

It's so important to understand and recognize when you're experiencing betrayal trauma. Often, it can be the underlying problem that rears its head in many of the symptoms listed above. But knowing this is what you're dealing with is the first step in your healing.[74]

Going through a betrayal, especially with your spouse, is an incredibly painful and often blind-siding experience. It's disorienting to discover that someone you trusted so deeply would choose to do something that caused you such intense pain.

But you can find healing from this experience. Here are three things to keep in mind as you begin the healing process:

BECOME AN EXPERT OF YOUR TRIGGERS

Even after incredible healing and post-traumatic growth occur, there are times when a betrayed spouse will experience something that triggers them or causes an emotional reaction. Here are a few suggestions that will help get through those triggers.

[74] A more exhaustive list can be found in the appendix at the back of the book.

First, it's important to remember that you won't be able to avoid all triggers in the beginning, simply because it's impossible to know exactly what will trigger you. But as you move forward, remember to identify what is causing you to feel triggered. Be mindful of your body and mind and how they're responding—what caused you to feel this way? When did you feel this way before?

Next, as you encounter a trigger, consider what follow-up might be needed—should you add boundaries to your life that weren't there before? Update a tool that you're using? Process the trauma with a counselor or a friend? These triggers are pointing out important things to you, and it's so important that you don't ignore them.

Finally, experiment with various stress relieving techniques and make a list of the ones that are helpful so you can quickly implement them when you're triggered. You can try deep breathing, yoga, lying under a weighted blanket, taking a warm bath, finding a safe person to talk to, go for a walk, do the breathing exercise mentioned in Chapter Eight, or listen to worship music. Or whatever works for you!

Triggers are important—don't ignore them. Instead, look for healthy ways to recover when they come up and always identify the thoughts and feelings associated with the trigger. Use a journal to write in until you identify those thoughts, feelings, and possibly a lie attached to that trigger.

BE RELENTLESS

Your healing and recovery are worth the work it takes, so you have to be relentless in pursuit of wellness. And this pursuit becomes easier when you keep all the various elements of your health in mind.

Just a few ways you can be relentless in seeking healing:

- Avoid alcohol and drugs. We want to replace unhelpful behaviors with helpful behaviors.
- Meditate on truth when shame lies creep into your mind.
- Change your environment if you're feeling triggered or tempted.
- Sleep, eat, and drink well.
- Stay physically active.
- Interact daily with the Lord.
- Journal regularly.
- Avoid unsafe people, places, events, or family functions.
- Eliminate triggers (social media, lingerie, sexual movies).
- Join a group or start counseling.
- Create a Recovery Action Plan or a Safety Action Plan.

Recovery and healing aren't just about the trauma you've just experienced. If you can seek health and healing in all the areas of your life—physical, mental, emotional, and spiritual—your journey to healing will be holistic and transformative in every way.

One of the items listed above is creating a Recovery Action Plan or a Safety Action Plan. What does that look like and why is it important?

THE RECOVERY ACTION PLAN—THE SAFETY ACTION PLAN

One of the most important steps a betrayed spouse can take is to create and implement what we call a Safety Action Plan.[75] This is a valuable tool for anyone wanting to take a proactive approach to recovery. It helps the betrayed spouse identify reasonable and necessary steps—focused on establishing safety and boundaries—should their spouse relapse. As the struggling spouse learns to walk in sobriety, the Recovery Action Plan helps them to transform addictive behaviors and provide healthy responses when challenges arise.

For many betrayed spouses, a Safety Action Plan is a helpful tool they create after discovery or disclosure, after they have processed the initial shock of betrayal and have engaged in counseling or a betrayal support group. However, for a betrayed spouse who is in an abusive situation—if they are experiencing emotional, physical, or sexual abuse—their safety is paramount. It's urgent that they take steps toward safety, first and foremost, and seek immediate help to get out of a potentially abusive situation.[76]

The primary goal of a Safety Action Plan is not to punish the spouse who is struggling but to establish safety and boundaries for the betrayed spouse and put things in place that will help them process any relapse in a positive, intentional manner.

---

[75] The **Safety Action Plan** is for the betrayed spouse. The **Recovery Action Plan** is for the struggling spouse. They are identical in many ways, but the language is catered to the individual filling out the plan. For more information on both plans, visit **https://puredesire.org/resources/**.

[76] If a betrayed partner is in an abusive relationship and in immediate danger, call 911 or the National Domestic Violence Hotline: 1-800-799-SAFE (7233).

Group leaders at Pure Desire have reported fewer relapses and a higher rate of sobriety among members who have developed a Recovery Action Plan/Safety Action Plan.

The purpose of the plan is to establish safety by identifying both natural and logical consequences if a relapse occurs—natural consequences are inevitable results of an addict's relapse, while logical consequences are suggested by the betrayed spouse or self-imposed by the addict. These aren't meant to be punitive but are intended to help the betrayed spouse feel safe, to have concrete steps in place in the event of relapse, and to work toward rebuilding trust and intimacy in the marriage. Ultimately, a Safety Action Plan empowers a betrayed spouse to focus on what they need for their healing. It is not their responsibility to control, cure, or fix the struggling spouse. The struggling spouse is fully responsible for their behaviors and ownership of their recovery.

It's important to remember that the Safety Action Plan is initially a plan for the benefit of the betrayed spouse and should be created by them. If, at some point along the way, the struggling spouse creates their own Recovery Action Plan, the two can be combined after a productive, non-reactionary conversation where each spouse shares their plan, and the betrayed spouse is given space to share their voice and how their spouse's behavior affects them.

One final thing to keep in mind before we go into the specifics of a Safety Action Plan: if your situation has escalated to the point of divorce or separation, your boundaries and safety steps will need to be redefined according to what the relationship is now and the desired outcome—reconciliation or divorce, with as little damage as possible. If your divorce is final, and you are experiencing stability and healthy boundaries, then you can use the Three Circles Exercise, included in an appendix in this book.

Every individual who completes an Action Plan should find trusted individuals to share their plan with—your group leader or members would be an ideal place to start. As we recommend for nearly every aspect of recovery, this isn't something you should try to do on your own.

Consequences. In the simplest terms, a consequence is an effect, result, or outcome of our actions. Consequences can be positive or negative, and natural (happen as a result of our actions) or logical (pre-planned ahead of time).

It is vital to the recovery process that consequences are predetermined and put in place in the event of relapse—suggested by the betrayed spouse for safety and stabilization or self-imposed by the struggling spouse. For the struggling spouse, this helps them weigh the outcome of their behavior and decide whether it's worth the risk. Often, when a struggling spouse takes responsibility for their behaviors and is committed to the recovery process, the pain of these consequences after a relapse can also create change in the punishment-reward center of their brain, helping them to connect painful consequences with a relapse. This makes a struggling person less likely to choose that path.

Consequences also help the addict own the effects of their behavior rather than withdrawing, blaming, hiding, lying, getting angry, or spiraling down into the depths of shame. When defined within a Safety Action Plan, consequences also help the betrayed spouse respond to their spouse's relapse in a nonemotional way: the struggling spouse's poor decisions are met, not primarily with anger or an emotional response, but with an action plan that was agreed on beforehand.

Predetermined consequences, discussed with wise counsel, reduce the need for the betrayed spouse to feel like a rescuer or the parent in the situation. The Safety Action Plan provides practical steps for the betrayed spouse to get the support they need to process the relapse and continue to move forward in their healing with boundaries in place. Relapse can be extremely painful for both spouses, and having consequences decided ahead of time allows everyone to enter into the plan with their eyes wide open, as opposed to letting emotions take the wheel and drive the way forward. And simply ignoring a relapse in order to find peace only fuels further relapse, not effective for long-term health or recovery.

Natural consequences versus logical consequences. We categorize the consequences of a relapse into two different areas: natural consequences and logical consequences. Natural consequences occur as a result of a choice without anyone imposing it. For example, if a struggling spouse relapses, a few natural consequences would be:

- Trust is broken, and their partner feels betrayed, causing them to be angry, reactive, and distant. These aren't consequences that have been agreed on beforehand—they simply happen naturally.
- A relapse can also create guilt or shame in the struggling spouse, causing them to feel distant from others.
- Another natural consequence can be the associated costs—an addiction will often cost valuable time, energy,

and money that's no longer available for more productive, positive purposes.

Logical consequences are reasonable and necessary outcomes either self-imposed or suggested by someone else. A Safety Action Plan is created by the betrayed spouse to initiate boundaries to establish safety. These are predetermined and agreed upon ahead of time. Some examples are:

- If the struggling spouse relapsed while watching YouTube videos alone late at night, the betrayed spouse will ask them to turn off all electronics after 10:30 pm and disable access to YouTube.
- If their cell phone continues to be a source for viewing inappropriate images, the betrayed spouse will ask them to disable the internet through their phone carrier.
- If their relapse involves flirting with others on social media, the betrayed spouse will ask them to close their account or only have a joint account with their spouse.

The Safety Action Plan is designed to give the betrayed spouse a clear picture of what they need in order to feel safe and process the pain of their spouse's relapse. This is a list of action steps the betrayed spouse will take to establish boundaries and continue moving forward in their healing. It also may include actions they would like to see in the struggling spouse's behaviors in order to regain trust and reestablish a safe space for intimacy.

If you're ready to begin thinking through your Safety Action Plan, here are a list of steps you can take to start the process:

Step One: Identify what constitutes a relapse in your mind. When has your spouse crossed a line that requires intentional recovery? And remember, the goal isn't to make your spouse perfect in every way! The goal is to identify which specific behaviors cause a fracture in your trust and intimacy.

Step Two: Determine in what time frame you will ask your spouse to share their relapse with you. We recommend sharing relapses within twenty-four hours. This step could also include details about what you will need when a relapse happens: time to process the relapse with a safe friend; childcare for __ amount of hours; initiate/invest in personal counseling.

Step Three: Write out the natural consequences of your spouse's behavior. Be clear about how their behavior impacts you.

Step Four: Write out logical consequences that focus on what you need to establish safety and boundaries. This may include steps that would help you see that your spouse recognizes the serious nature of their actions. (A list of potential natural and logical consequences that spouses have incorporated into their plan can be found in the appendix.)

Step Five: Make a list of steps you will need to personally take in order to find safety and stability, and be ready to fully engage in the relationship.

Step Six: Finally, describe your desired outcome for creating this plan. It's important to remember the goal of a Safety Action Plan is not to punish the struggling spouse or to add more shame and guilt, but to keep you both focused on what steps will be needed to rebuild trust, should a relapse occur.

In the event of a relapse, review your written Safety Action Plan and implement it immediately! When lying, blaming, hiding, and withdrawal take place after a relapse, it will only make recovery more difficult and increase the likelihood of multiple relapses. In order to encourage your spouse to come clean right away, consequences should be greater if the relapse isn't disclosed within twenty-four hours.

One last note for the betrayed spouse: rebuilding trust and intimacy takes intentionality and time. When trust is broken, the rebuilding process can be a long journey. It's important for the struggling spouse to be patient in reestablishing that trust, even while actively working on their own recovery. Before full disclosure, there were probably many lies and deceptions taking place in your marriage, so it's natural for trust to be difficult. The betrayed spouse will need to begin seeing things that help them start trusting again. The struggling spouse's willingness to do the things necessary for the betrayed spouse to feel vulnerable and safe enough to trust again is going to be the key to marital health and reconciliation.

When the struggling spouse shows they are absolutely committed to the recovery process, including what is being asked of them in the Safety Action Plan—even without anyone else's insistence or pressure—they can begin building trust after a relapse.

ONE-SIDED HEALING

One word of encouragement—it's normal for the struggling spouse and the betrayed spouse to start their healing at different times. It's normal for one spouse to feel extremely motivated to "fix" things immediately while the other spouse feels more reluctant or wants nothing to do with it.

If you're the one who's ready to do the work, the best thing you can do is not let your spouse's mindset discourage you and get busy doing the work you need to do for your own healing and transformation. If they're not leaning into healing, your only job is you. Whether you're the struggler or the one who has been betrayed, healing is available to you!

Engagement in group and healing activities is so important for the struggling spouse—they often get distracted by the exhilarating freedom that comes after confession, thinking they're in a better place than they actually are. Healing, true transformation, takes longer than most of us think, and if we don't commit to the required work and take the time to change the way we live, a relapse is almost inevitable.

Besides, just because you're no longer acting out doesn't mean your spouse can see a change in you. If the husband had an addiction to porn, and now he's no longer engaging in that, his wife won't see a difference since he was doing all of those things in secret before! I remember my wife (Nick) saying to me, "I couldn't see the things you were doing in secret and now I can't see the things you're abstaining from." I realized that just as I focused on stopping my old behaviors, I also needed to focus on new behaviors that would give my spouse tangible evidence that change was taking place. How I used devices, how I engaged with our kids, and how I treated her all became much more helpful barometers for my wife to see that change was taking place!

The struggler's life, on the outside, might appear exactly the same, so if he or she is not going to group or doing the homework, it's difficult for trust to be rebuilt. That takes time and the struggling spouse needs to keep doing the work and focusing on inner transformation. If they're experiencing inner transformation, eventually their spouse will notice the difference.

There's one story of a couple where the struggling spouse committed to doing the work while the betrayed spouse didn't want anything to do with it. She didn't want to join a group. But then she saw how hard her husband was working, how his relationship with Jesus was growing by leaps and bounds, and she realized she didn't want to miss any opportunity to experience deep healing, so she joined a group too.

"He was running hard after Jesus," she said. "I didn't want to get left behind. I wanted to work on myself, too."

If you're truly growing and transforming, whichever side of the equation you're on, that will speak the loudest to your spouse.

A Helpful Warning ...

Even after all of this work, it is possible things won't work out. When you decide to do the work, only one thing is guaranteed—your relationship with this person will never be the same again! When one person decides to change, it's impossible for a marriage to continue on as it was. In these kinds of betrayal situations, this is good news.

After all, it takes two spouses to decide they want to move forward after a betrayal, and it takes two spouses working very hard to get through the required journey of healing. Sometimes, this proves too much. Sometimes, the struggling spouse doesn't see a problem with what they're doing.

It's possible that at the end of betrayal, even when you do all the necessary work to move toward healing and reconciliation, divorce or separation becomes unavoidable. This can be a heartbreaking reality to face, made even more difficult when children are involved.

But even if you're in a place where your spouse has left or you've been divorced, attend to the work in front of you. Whether you end up living the rest of your life single, remarry your spouse, or end up in another marriage someday, you have work to do to become a better person and follower of Christ. It will take hard work, but you will experience the freedom and purpose God wants you to walk in! Trust God with the results of your relationships and you'll become a version of yourself that feels more at peace. And this will be a good thing for the marriage you're in, or, if they insist on leaving, it will be a good thing for any relationships you enter down the road.

CHAPTER TEN

HEALING FOR THE COUPLE AND THE FAMILY

One of the most common lies that can haunt the thinking of those struggling with compulsive sexual behavior is that my actions aren't hurting anyone. As we talked about earlier, the reality is that these "secret" behaviors—these unspoken areas of our lives that need healing—have a huge impact on those around us, even before we confess or open up about what we've been doing. But when we decide to finally come clean, the need for healing becomes obvious.

Perhaps no one is more affected by the struggler's journey than their own family. The betrayed spouse, after they find out what has been going on, has an entire world to reorient. If the couple has children, they will begin to realize that something is going on, and depending on their ages and the level of disclosure, they'll need to begin processing their own emotions. As parents, we can believe we are doing a good job of protecting our kids from knowing what's going on. We don't want to instill fear or worry in our kids. But even if our kids don't understand exactly what is going on, they *feel* that something is different.

When my husband and I (Ashley) were early on in our recovery and healing journey, our two younger kids knew that we went to a men's and women's group, but we didn't talk about any of our struggles in front of them. One night, at dinner, my daughter was praying (she was probably around 5 years old) and she said, "God, thank you for this dinner and please help my dad to stop lying." My husband, Jon, and I could not believe she picked up on that! Our kids can assume that we are distant or irritable because we don't want to spend time with them. They can start to believe they have done something wrong. We need to reassure them that their instincts are correct, that there *is* something going on, *and* it isn't their fault.

The best case scenario is when healing, which starts out as an individual's journey, turns into something the entire family begins to seek. A redemption story is the best kind of story, but it only happens after devastation occurs and then everyone involved commits to bettering themselves and their relationships.

But what could healing look like?

True healing?

That moment of disclosure may feel like life has ended, but if the struggler and their spouse are willing to seek healing, it might be the beginning of a journey that leads to a stronger, more resilient, more beautiful relationship, in all of its many facets—physically, mentally, emotionally, and spiritually. Over time, as the struggler continues to live in recovery and pursue health, it's the kind of healing that inspires those around them—their children, their extended family, and their friends. People begin to see everything that is being overcome—not perfection, but true transformation and real change—and they begin to envision it for themselves.

- *If he can get freedom from that porn addiction, then maybe I can too.*
- *If she can work through her unfaithfulness to her husband, maybe I can too.*
- *If they can make it as a couple even after going through everything they've gone through, then maybe our marriage can survive too.*

We've seen it happen many, many times.

Marcus and Jada were married for more than a decade when things fell apart.

Jada learned from an early age how to fake her way through life. She had a lot of wounds from her childhood that she brought into the marriage, and some of the ways she learned to cope that came with those wounds led her into a life of secret infidelity. Sometimes she couldn't believe the things she was doing, and all behind Marcus' back, but she was used to maintaining a false veneer while other things went on below the surface, so in some ways this was no different. She simply kept pretending.

Marcus thought everything was fine and that they had a great marriage. They had two beautiful little girls. Life, to him, was going on more or less as a life should. But it wasn't what it appeared to be.

Jada reached a point in her life when she became exhausted by the charade, when she got so sick of the lying and faking life. But she wasn't sure how to move out of it. She talked to a friend who encouraged her to tell Marcus what was going on—even if there was only a glimmer of hope that they could survive it, wouldn't the marriage be better on the other side, where they could live in honesty with each other? It all sounded good, and she longed to live in that place of honesty, transparency, and freedom.

But she just wasn't sure how to tell him.

At about the same time that Jada was having these conversations with her friend, Marcus was having his own internal conversations with God. He had absolutely no inclination about Jada's unfaithfulness to him. Then he went on a hunting trip with his friends.

One day while he was climbing a mountain in the woods, hiking to the same spot every day, he was just thinking about how tough it was to get to the top of that ridge every morning. It took a lot of effort, but it was worth it—making it up there, finding his quiet spot.

And that's when God first warned him that something was coming in his life.

If you think climbing this mountain is tough, what you are about to endure will be even tougher.

That feeling settled in, that something unimaginable was on the horizon. It unsettled him. He wondered what it could possibly be.

Then, on the drive home, he was blindsided by this idea that he couldn't quite shake: he knew when he got home he needed to ask her if she was being unfaithful.

No, he thought. *It can't be possible. Why would I even think that?*

When he walked in the door from the hunting trip, he was confronted by this sense that Jada wasn't that excited to see him, and that hurt. When he saw how she greeted a friend who came over to pick something up, he could see the difference—with Marcus, she seemed very disinterested, and there wasn't much of a light in her eyes, but with friends, she was enthusiastic.

Why hadn't he noticed this before?

Again, the nudge to ask her if she was being unfaithful.

Their girls were in the bath one evening when he finally worked up the courage. And even when the words came out, he still thought it was crazy, why was he even asking her this.

"Have you been unfaithful to me?"

When the words came out, she looked up at him.

She nodded her head, yes. And things got very dark for Marcus.

This can be one of the most crucial points in a relationship—when one spouse confesses to the other about what has been going on, when they finally admit to the porn addiction or the infidelity or the compulsive sexual behaviors, everyone in the relationship has to decide if they want to give up or if they want to pursue healing.

One thing to remember—the desire for healing might not happen right away. There are a lot of emotions to experience, a lot of questions and heartache to address. But at some point, if the marriage is going to make it, the question has to be addressed.

It's reminiscent of the passage in John 5:5–6. An invalid had been lying beside the pool of Bethesda for thirty-eight years, and when Jesus walked up to him, saw him lying there in his condition, Jesus asked him, "Do you want to get well?"

That, often, is the question that each person in the marriage must ask themselves.

Do I want to get well?

Marcus was devastated by the news. He went three days without sleeping, and lost twenty pounds in a month. He knew he needed to eat, but he just couldn't. He developed an eye twitch from the anxiety of the situation. He wasn't sure if he even believed in panic attacks before Jada's confession, but he started having them. He felt himself getting more and more depressed.

How had they gotten to this point? How had they managed to grow so far apart without him even realizing it? And more pressing: did he even want to fight for this marriage after such painful dishonesty and unfaithfulness? He didn't know what the future held, and he moved out.

Meanwhile, Jada was grasping at straws. If she wanted to stay in the marriage, where would she even begin? What would that look like? How could they do it? Could Marcus ever forgive her?

Could God ever forgive her?

Could she forgive herself for the pain she had caused this man she loved?

The temptation then was to walk away—it felt easier to start again with someone else than to put in the work and the hard days. She knew it was not going to be an easy road, winning back Marcus' trust, recovering their marriage from the rubble.

But Jada remembered what her friend had said—if there is a glimmer of hope, then it's worth fighting for. She started opening herself up to the possibility of a healed marriage, of a new journey with Marcus. She read books on it and listened to podcasts. After reading a book about a wife who had an affair and found healing, she reached out to the author.

"This is my situation," she wrote. "What do I do? What do you recommend?"

The author's response?

"You need to get in touch with Pure Desire. You need to join a group. You need to get counseling."

It took her some time to get there, and all along Marcus kept telling her, "I don't know how, but someday I'll forgive you. I want this marriage, and I want you, and I think you're worth fighting for."

That glimmer of hope.

She decided she would fight for their marriage.

Prior to joining Pure Desire, they had been going to a psychologist for marriage counseling, but it didn't seem all that helpful, especially after Jada's confession, because the psychologist didn't specialize in infidelity, recovery, or sexual addiction. Jada decided to give a Pure Desire *Unraveled* online group a try. She did not know what to expect or what she was getting into.

She had no idea the classes would go on for nine or ten months, but that's how long it can take to adjust how we live and begin making permanent changes to neural pathways. One of the biggest surprises to her was how the group taught her to do new things, even in her thirties.

For example, learning how to be honest again.

She was surprised at how often she wasn't completely honest, how much integrity it took to become an honest person, and how important it was in the recovery process.

When it came time for Jada to share her story with the other women in the group, she was nervous and scared. But everyone was in it together, and the layout of the material allowed for the women to slowly unpack their experiences. As the groups went on, Jada learned who she was, how she got to where she was. And in turn that gave her the courage she needed to share her story little by little.

This was such a beautiful counterbalance to the pattern of hiding that Jada had created for herself. She practiced hiding and wearing masks until she became an expert at it—whether it was in her marriage or as the leader of a life group or a moms' group. She never felt safe to completely be herself.

Until she went to her Pure Desire group. There, for the first time, she could bring all of herself, and when she did she was accepted with love and open arms. Her vulnerability was encouraged and valued.

But healing as a couple isn't always easy or straightforward. Sometimes, when Jada was at her group, Marcus was tempted to wonder, *What is she even talking about? Is she talking about me? Does she miss me?* And when he allowed himself to go down that road, he could feel himself spiraling.

Yet when he was in a healthier space, instead of those questions, he chose to see what was happening right in front of him: she was taking the time to try and change things; she was doing homework that was helping them gain back their intimacy and love for each other; she was working on her own healing and practicing peace.

He could see that truth-telling entered their everyday lives. It was making a difference.

They each had days where they wanted to leave or where they wanted to stay. Where they wanted to keep trying or when they wanted to give up.

But seeing the growth they were both experiencing gave them another small glimmer of hope. And they kept trying.

After the confession, the devastation moved out in concentric circles, affecting everyone else in their lives.

The same happened with healing.

Soon, they started to see their daughters picking up on their newfound commitment to honesty. Marcus and Jada learned how to ask their kids how they were doing, really ask, and they started getting answers besides, "Fine." They both became better parents, which changed their family dynamic for the better.

They were able to empathize with their kids, where before they might have ignored them or told them everything was okay or to toughen up. They cleaned up the television shows and music their kids were taking in, and they started to see honesty show up in the interactions their girls had at school.

They've created a family code that operates on kindness, love, forgiveness, honesty, and generosity. Their relationships have deepened.

And the healing kept moving out. Jada took her healing and decided to look into leading a Pure Desire group. She was nervous about that first night: *What would they say? How would people respond to her? What if they were the only couple who was willing to admit to having "real problems"?*

Jada started the group by sharing her own story, walking people through what they had experienced and how they had found healing. And almost immediately others began opening up about their own areas where they needed help. The women started taking steps toward healing.

And because they were all sharing in-depth with each other, their relationships deepened. Healing was paid forward to others. More and more people experienced it, simply because of Marcus and Jada's original decision to be honest with one another and to make their recovery and healing the most important priority. To this day, they have encouraged countless couples as they have publicly shared their story of healing and encouraged others to take the same healing journey they did. The legacy of their healing continues to grow!

PART FOUR

WHAT'S NEXT

CHAPTER ELEVEN

THE POWER OF AN INTENTIONAL RECOVERY GROUP

The group aspect of Pure Desire really can be the most beautiful part of the experience. The homework is important; going to an outside counselor or therapist can give you added insight on yourself and your relationships. But it's in the group that we often find true love and acceptance for the first time in our lives.

That said, because groups are so important, it's also crucial that certain things are done to build the kind of groups that are helpful. We've probably all been in some kind of a group that became toxic—maybe a classroom setting, or a sports team, or even a church body. We know how detrimental an unhealthy group can be during normal seasons of life—a bad group can have even more negative effects when we're trying to journey through extremely difficult spaces.

We also know what it's like to be in a good, solid group that doesn't produce change. Doing a book study together can be a great activity. Like Brother Finney began in small groups hundreds of years ago, gathering weekly to walk through a set of questions is healthy.[77] But without a significant plan specific to recovery, we have found that many sincere, "good" groups create very little, if any, true change.

The guidelines we've created for our groups didn't come from paid focus groups or geniuses in the field. They didn't come from what other people said we should do or create. These guidelines have really risen out of years and years of experience, seeing what has worked the best for the individual and the group, and then talking to group leaders all around the world and seeing what has worked the best for them.

Also, we don't normally refer to these as rules, but more as a basic structure meant to create a space that fosters trust. A group with guidelines becomes a safe place we can go to each week, knowing we've agreed to certain things. A group that doesn't follow the guidelines? Well, we'll talk more about that in a minute.

If you join a group or become a group leader, hopefully you don't have to learn these lessons the hard way. The guidelines we've created will help you avoid some of the many mistakes that have been made in the past and pave a way to a successful, life-transforming group.

So, here are the guidelines that have created such success for men and women in Pure Desire groups:

---

[77] "Charles Grandison Finney," *Wikipedia, The Free Encyclopedia*, 7 June 2025, **https://en.wikipedia.org/wiki/Charles_Grandison_Finney#**.

Confidentiality. What is said in group is presented in trust and confidence, and this has to be given the utmost consideration. Whatever is said in the group stays in the group. Information about someone's story should never be shared without that person's consent, even with spouses. In order to protect this confidentiality, the group is never open to guests or visitors, and if someone new wants to join the group midway through, they need to go directly to the group leader.

Maintaining a place of confidentiality is one of the biggest factors in encouraging people to be open and honest. If people know that what they say will not leave the room, it gives them a greater sense of freedom to share their story, which in turn creates camaraderie in the room and allows for greater healing and transformation.

It's even important to not talk widely about who is in your group—they may not feel comfortable with others knowing they're part of the group. Confidentiality is a foundation to a good group.

High-level commitment. For the group experience to be transforming, we ask group members to make this commitment their priority. Other than family emergencies, or truly unavoidable work commitments, group members are expected to attend every meeting. When we have this level of sincerity to our healing, it becomes part of how we change. The truth is, we often get out of group what we put into it, so we are bold to ask group members up front to make this a top-shelf priority for this season. It could mean you lay down a hobby for a time, or that the kids play fewer sports, or that you back out of other conflicting commitments. We have seen these kinds of decisions routinely lead people to the level of sincerity they need to experience deep change!

Respect others. Respecting each person in the group is another important step to take, and this involves self-focus, listening respectfully, and limiting your sharing. When we say self-focus, we mean speaking only for yourself and avoiding giving advice.

Listening means allowing others the time they need to formulate their responses, not cutting them off, interrupting, or finishing their thoughts for them. Sometimes, if we cut someone off, it literally cuts off their ability to experience the healing they need.

Limiting sharing means sticking to the time you've been given to answer the question posed and avoiding following rabbit trails. It's important that each group member has time to share, and you show respect for others by not taking over a meeting with your own stories.

Commitment to accountability. It's so important that each group member makes the group a priority, letting your leader know if for some reason you can't attend. Contact other group members three times each week, and also contact a group member if you experience a relapse. Finally, if you feel uncomfortable with anything about the group, talk with the leader of the group.

The group leaders, in turn, must be accountable to the church organizing the group, adhering to all leadership requirements of the church and its policies. Leaders should also meet with other church leaders at least once each quarter to report successes and challenges.

A Note on True Accountability: It's important to recognize the difference between true accountability and backward accountability. The typical church accountability group operates in a way where the one looking for accountability normally says something like, "I give you permission to check on me anytime! Keep me accountable." This is backward, because the person looking to change has given responsibility for that change to someone else. Now it's the other person's fault if they don't call or check in or are too busy to ask how the person is doing.

True accountability puts the responsibility in the hands of the person seeking change. In true accountability, the person seeking change says, "I am committing to you that I will check in with you and take responsibility to tell you how I am doing specifically in the areas I'm feeling challenged." At the end of every Pure Desire lesson, we make a commitment to change: we each say what our greatest challenge to sobriety will be in the coming week, what our plan is to deal with it proactively, and who we will check in with (and when) to communicate how we're doing.

Backward accountability rarely works, because the person outside the situation simply isn't as concerned about seeing change as the struggling individual is—true accountability puts the responsibility back in the hands of the struggler and gives them the tools they need to truly be accountable to those in their group.

Complete the homework. Maybe you don't want to call it homework? I know that for those of us who struggled in school, homework became a word that reinforced all the ways we were failing during adolescence, or it reminds you of getting graded and not hitting a high enough standard.

Perhaps you want to call it self-discovery or answering questions about your life. Whatever you call it, it's important to remember you're not being evaluated or graded.

But this homework is important, because it facilitates your journey to healing. Allow twenty to thirty minutes each day to complete it, and those in the group who write it down have the opportunity to participate in sharing and making a contribution to the group. Writing it down is an important part of the process—it gives the group member the opportunity to think through their experience, and then when it's time for them to share in the group, they can read through their answer. This keeps them from meandering on and on, something that takes time away from other group members.

Covenant to Contend. For addiction recovery groups, we ask group members to make a public commitment that is witnessed by the entire group, stating your dedication to the process of your healing.

Memo of Understanding. Finally, it's crucial—mandatory even—that each group member understands and agrees to the purpose and parameters of Pure Desire groups, along with the moral and ethical obligations of group leaders outlined in the Memo of Understanding. This document must be signed before anyone can join the group.[78]

Whenever a group is launching, it's important that these guidelines are introduced and agreed to up front, because that makes all the difference. The last thing you want to do is realize there's some negative behavior taking place halfway through and then try to address it and change the behavior. Whenever we have a group that's having trouble, if we walk through the guidelines we'll usually find one that isn't being followed, or perhaps one that the leader is being a bit lax about.

So what happens when a guideline is broken?

The first step is to address it with the entire group as a sort of reminder. Maybe a few people aren't doing their homework, so for the first instance of this we don't single them out, but we'll remind the group, "Hey, it's important to do your homework."

If it happens again, we will pull that person aside at some point and remind them of the guideline they're breaking, why it's important,

[78] More information about joining a Pure Desire group can be found in the NEXT STEPS section of this book.

and make sure they can commit to following it. This isn't meant to shame or degrade them or their effort, but it is simply a reminder to them about why that particular guideline is important.

After that, if they keep missing that guideline, the conversation gets tough. We ask them if they're sure this group is right for them—maybe they need to step aside and join a different group in a different season of their life, perhaps when they feel more equipped to adhere to the group guidelines.

These kinds of conversations aren't fun, but they're necessary for the integrity of the group. What's comfortable and easy is what got many of us into this situation in the first place, so groups are a place where we can begin to make a change, choosing what's good and necessary over what's comfortable and easy.

WHAT ABOUT THE BIG PICTURE?

People will often ask if we think we're making progress in eliminating pornography from our culture. If we work hard enough, if we talk about it enough, if we legislate in the right way, can we be successful in a war against porn?

The statistics aren't in our favor.

The porn industry brings in more money than the combined revenues of ABC, NBC, and CBS, more than the income of the NFL, NBA, and MLB, generating somewhere between $15 billion and $97 billion every year.[79] More people watch porn every month than those who watch Netflix, Amazon Prime, and X combined. In 2023, in just one month, a major porn site had 700,000,000 more views than Amazon.[80] Yes, that's the right amount of zeros—seven hundred million!

There's so much money in porn, and it plays so well into how our bodies are hardwired, that it's hard to imagine eradicating it completely. Don't misinterpret what we're saying—we support people trying to make positive changes, such as beefing up age verification on porn sites and outlawing prostitution rings that are trafficking people. But at the end of the day we believe true transformation and change comes from the inside out, not from crusading to eradicate pornography from culture.

Christian history shows a group of people on the fringes of their culture being radically transformed by God, and then the culture recognizing that these Christians are living out a better way. It's the story of the early Christians in Jerusalem who shared their possessions and lived in a beautiful community. It's the story of the Christians in Rome, persecuted but still dedicating their lives to helping the poor and sick, the weak and abandoned. It's the story of Christians in the Dark Ages who sat with those dying from the contagious Black Death.

---

[79] Lyndon Azcuna, "The Porn Pandemic," *LifePlan*, October 28, 2021, **https://www.lifeplan.org/the-porn-pandemic/**.

[80] Nichole K. McNichols, "How Many People Actually Watch Porn?" *Psychology Today*, September 25, 2023, **https://www.psychologytoday.com/us/blog/everyone-on-top/202309/how-much-porn-do-americans-really-watch**.

And it's the revolution that's needed in our own culture, where Christians don't get lost in the normalization of porn and a warped sexuality, where we rise up showing a better way to live. The testimony we can offer is that of being dedicated to our spouse, of living in sexual health, and of doing the tough inner work to remain faithful to this calling.

The best way to change the culture is to change our marriages, our families, and ourselves for the better, to follow Jesus more closely, and to shine bright in the darkness—not just talk about it but display it in the way we live.

The best way to change the culture is to introduce people to meaningful groups where they can do the work, share their stories, experience true love and acceptance, and undergo radical transformation. When our culture sees this, it's attracted to it. That's what will bring about lasting change.

CHAPTER TWELVE

YOU CAN DO THIS

Do you remember Kurt, the church leader who had first encountered porn when he was 8 years old, something that led to a lifetime of compulsive sexual addiction? He tried to quit dozens of times on his own, and sometimes he could go a couple months, but it never stuck. He always ended up going back.

Until he found his way into a Pure Desire group. The road wasn't easy—after his confession, his marriage hit some of the toughest waters they had ever gone through, and he voluntarily stepped down from his church leadership position. For a while, he wondered if confessing and entering the Pure Desire program had been the right thing to do.

But now, three years after entering the group, he's leading Pure Desire groups of his own, helping others to find freedom. His wife is walking alongside betrayed spouses who don't know what to do after receiving these confessions. The amount of transformation that has entered the world is incredible, all because of Kurt's decision to tell the truth and stop living a lie.

Kurt found hope, healing, and freedom.

Remember Keisha, the girl who could never (in her words) "be good enough," who left her church because she felt she had more in common with her friends outside of the church, woke up one Sunday morning, hungover again, regretting decisions she had made again? She wondered what it would take to turn her life around—and if it was even possible.

She dragged herself to church that morning and it just so happened to be a Sunday morning when the church was introducing Pure Desire groups. She heard what they said about compulsive sexual behaviors and realized for the first time that's what she was struggling with—that was her. It was an addiction.

That evening, before she could stop herself, she had fired off an email to the church contact about joining a group, and it was with a fair amount of fear and trepidation that she attended the first meeting. What an incredible surprise when she almost immediately fell in love with most of the other women in the group, women who told stories similar to hers, women who had the same struggles and desires for freedom!

She is still working her way through the program but has already seen incredible transformation. The effective accountability in the group has been just the tool she needed to start making positive changes, and her deepening relationship with Christ is helping her understand that His love for her isn't dependent on anything—not her behavior, not her choices, not her way of life. It's this unconditional love that is freeing her.

Keisha found hope, healing, and freedom.

Remember Bill, the older veteran who thought that if he told anyone about his habit, his life would fall apart?

He waited and waited. His wife passed away. His children got jobs in other parts of the country. And he found himself looking back on a long life, some good, some bad. He had some regrets.

He eventually found his way to a Pure Desire group, and he, too, discovered a path to freedom. But in some ways, he felt like it was too late—he wishes he would have gone through the program when his wife was still living. He wonders about the level of intimacy and friendship they might have discovered if he had just been honest. He's glad to be done with the compulsive behaviors, but he also can't help but think of his wife. He wonders if maybe she would have had more grace for him than he imagined. He wonders if she had already known.

There is a new way of life for Bill now, but fear stole years of freedom from him. He just wishes he would have had the courage to do it sooner.

Bill eventually found hope, healing, and freedom.

If you're the one who's struggling or who has emerged from a life of struggling, remember this: you can be a beacon of light for countless others who are currently caught up in the midst of their struggle and feel very little hope. As someone seeking transformation, you can shine the light of God's goodness; you can show a very good gospel to those who feel lost. So many are drowning in the sexual aspect of their lives, hopelessly addicted to porn, or going through a string of broken relationships.

You can be an example of freedom that will draw people to Christ.

Satan can only trap us one person at a time, because the enemy's greatest influence comes in secrecy and shame. Some of our most addictive transgressions happen in secret and isolation and loneliness. It's a form of subtraction, where we are separated from the community one by one.

But healing happens in multiplication, in communities where many lives are changed.

How many do you hope to impact with your story in the coming year?

I (Nick) was asked the question during my recovery. How many people did I hope to impact with my story in the future? I said that I hoped to impact at least five in the first year, perhaps fifty in the next five years. But after five years I looked back and realized I had led seven groups that included thirty-five people; I had shared my story with my church (around 300 people); and I had spoken at several conferences. I had probably shared my story with 10,000 people—not all of them experienced freedom or transformation, but I'm sure many did.

Satan can only get us one at a time, but when we experience transformation, we can bring many, many more along to healing with us.

We share a story in one of our courses about college students who were paid $20 as part of a study and invited into a room to work on a problem. Then a separate group of college students were invited to work on the same problem, but they were told that their work would help provide support for Alzheimer's patients.

The outcome and effort of the people in the second group, who were motivated by the prospect of helping others, went way beyond those in the first group.

So, if you're exploring or entering recovery, keep this in mind—who in your life is going to be helped? What will this work you're doing mean for your kids, their future spouses, their future children and grandchildren? What will this transformation mean for your community? Your church? Your friends?

You can either enter recovery thinking you're just in it for yourself, or you can start by understanding that many, many other lives will be transformed by the choices you make, for better or for worse. It's an ongoing process that will spread out to so many others.

For the betrayed spouse, we offer these words of encouragement: because of what we've witnessed during all these years, our prayer is that you will experience healing and freedom. This might sound impossible right now, and we understand! Often betrayed partners can feel chained to their spouse's addictions or compulsive sexual behaviors. Plus you might depend on your spouse for financial or physical security. Your spouse's poor decisions can leave you feeling like you have no way out, that you're trapped in this incredibly difficult situation.

But there is hope and joy and purpose found in post-traumatic growth. So many of the people we've seen go through this trauma and healing end up saying they're thankful for where they're at—not thankful they had to go through the trauma, but they're thankful they were able to become a stronger, more confident person than they ever were before.

As a betrayed spouse, we can also remember that God has never promised us a trial-free existence, but that regardless of what comes our way, we can live with a sense of freedom and hope and joy.

It is difficult, when you're in the midst of compulsive sexual behaviors, to imagine a life where you are completely free of those things. You've tried to quit so many times. You're afraid to tell the truth because you don't want to hurt those closest to you. What if you can't overcome it? But just like Kurt, Keisha, and Bill, and the thousands of others like them who find hope, healing, and freedom through a Pure Desire group each year, you can learn to walk in a new, life-giving way.

There is a pathway to freedom.

It's a journey worth taking.

What are you waiting for?

> *Therefore, since we are surrounded by such a great cloud of witnesses, let us throw off every encumbrance and the sin that so easily entangles, and let us run with endurance the race set out for us. Let us fix our eyes on Jesus, the author and perfecter of our faith, who for the joy set before Him endured the cross, scorning its shame, and sat down at the right hand of the throne of God.*
>
> **HEBREWS 12:1–2 (BSB)**

NEXT STEPS

Are you ready to take your next step? Whether you're a person who struggles with pornography and compulsive sexual behaviors, a spouse who is experiencing betrayal trauma, or a person who feels called to help others, we have a next step for you.

Pure Desire offers safe, confidential online groups and counseling for those who are struggling or experiencing betrayal trauma. We also have resources for those who want to help others find hope, healing, and freedom.

FOR THOSE STRUGGLING

For men struggling with pornography and compulsive sexual behavior we recommend joining a **Seven Pillars of Freedom** group. For single, college-aged men, we recommend joining a **Living Free** group. Recovery and healing happens best in a safe community with others on the same healing journey, where you can process and make sense of your story, and have a clear pathway to freedom.

For women who struggle with pornography, love, sex, or relationship issues, we recommend joining an **Unraveled** group. For single, college-aged women, we recommend joining an **Authentically You** group. In this safe, grace-filled environment, women can process their past pain and trauma, reclaim their identity in Christ, and learn what it looks like to live in sexual and relational health.

FOR BETRAYED PARTNERS

For women who have experienced betrayal trauma, we recommend joining a **Betrayal & Beyond** group. In this safe community with other women who are on the same healing journey, women will learn to create boundaries and safety, understand how to calm their mind when triggered, gain a greater understanding of addictive behaviors so they are equipped to make informed decisions, and experience the hope found in healing.

FIND A GROUP

To find the best group for you, either locally or a Pure Desire online group, visit **puredesire.org/join-a-group** or reach out to our groups team at **onlinegroups@puredesire.org**.

CLINICAL COUNSELING

While starting with a group may be the best next step for many, it's not always the best next step for others. Those who have experienced past trauma and abuse often find personal counseling the best place to start. Our clinical team specializes in guiding clients through the process of overcoming compulsive sexual behavior and healing from betrayal trauma. Our counseling programs are biblically based and clinically informed.

We have male and female clinicians who work with individuals, as well as male/female clinician teams who work with couples. Our clinical teams are certified through the International Institute for Trauma and Addiction Professionals (IITAP) as Certified Sex Addiction Therapists (CSAT) or Pastoral Sex Addiction Professionals (PSAP). Each clinical team has years of pastoral ministry experience, allowing them to counsel from a biblical and theological perspective.

Since we offer counseling via online video conferencing, you can receive counseling from anywhere in the world. For more information on the Pure Desire Counseling Programs, visit **puredesire.org/counseling**.

HELPING OTHERS

For those who have been called to help others struggling with pornography, compulsive sexual behavior, and betrayal trauma, we recommend going through ***Sexual Integrity 101***. This 8-part video course will educate and equip you to have a greater understanding of:

- compulsive sexual behaviors and the addiction cycle
- the brain and neuroscience behind addictive behaviors
- how compulsive sexual behaviors impact relationships and family dynamics
- the way shame fuels addictive behaviors
- practical tools and strategies that lead to lasting healing

To learn more about *Sexual Integrity 101*, visit **puredesire.org/shop/sexual-integrity-101-video-course**.

If you're interested in starting a healing ministry in your church, we're here to help! You can reach out to our groups team at **groups@puredesire.org** or learn more about leading a Pure

Desire group through the ***Group Leader Training***: **puredesire.org/shop/group-leader-training**. This video course will equip you to effectively lead life-changing Pure Desire groups.

FREE RESOURCES AND TOOLS

If you don't find yourself in the categories listed above but want more information about Pure Desire, who we are and what we do, we have free resources for you: the Pure Desire Podcast, the Unfiltered Podcast, blogs, and ebooks. All of these resources, and additional tools, can be found at **puredesire.org/resources**.

Wherever you're at on your journey, we're here to help.

APPENDIX

SAFETY ACTION PLAN: NATURAL AND LOGICAL CONSEQUENCES

When creating a Safety Action Plan: Here are a few examples of natural consequences that occur when a spouse relapses—we encourage the betrayed spouse to write out their own natural consequences on a separate sheet of paper:

- I feel devalued, objectified, not worth fighting for, and unprotected. I no longer feel stability in our marriage.
- My trust is broken and I feel vulnerable and exposed—I have a difficult time discerning what is true in our marriage and if my spouse is serious about recovery and our relationship.
- I feel emotionally disconnected from my spouse and no longer feel secure enough to be close and intimate.
- When my spouse lies about a relapse (including delayed confession), it creates anxiety in me that causes me to wonder what else in our marriage is a lie. I begin to replay the days and months in my head, trying to figure out what signs I missed. I start to doubt my own intuition about something being "off" in our marriage.
- I compare myself to the person(s) my spouse fantasizes about and feel less attractive.
- I feel like I'm not good enough.

- My spouse is contributing to an industry that destroys society and families.
- My relationship with God grows distant because of the anger and isolation I feel.
- I'm not engaged with my children because my mind is preoccupied.
- I'm distracted at work and become unproductive.
- I feel pain and insecurity.
- I receive less of my spouse's energy and attention.
- I become angry and, at times, irrational in my words and treatment of my spouse.

This is an incomplete list. It's so important that both spouses write out a list of the natural consequences of a relapse. As we mentioned earlier, knowing the consequences can go a long way toward keeping a relapse from happening.

What about logical consequences? How do we go about setting those? Just remember that these examples are tied to an action and help both spouses recognize the connection of a relapse to its corresponding consequence. After reading through these examples, write out your own logical consequences separately:

- Because I feel devalued and objectified after a relapse occurs, I will need space and time to process what happened. I will ask my spouse to sleep in another room, on the couch, or on the floor for ______ days/weeks until I can feel stability again and ready to move forward with emotional intimacy and then physical intimacy. If relapse occurs again, the number of days out of the bed will double.

- If flirting or inappropriate behavior with a coworker takes place, I will ask my spouse to not travel alone with a coworker of the opposite sex. I will ask my spouse to keep conversations to work topics only. If relapse continues to occur or if physical boundaries are crossed, I will ask my spouse to seek other employment or moving departments will be necessary.
- If my spouse misuses social media, I will ask them to delete any triggering person from their contacts and stay off social media for one month. If they keep repeating this behavior, then I will ask them to delete their social media accounts indefinitely until they have established six months of sobriety in all areas of addiction.
- If my spouse views pornography on their phone, I will ask them to block internet access on the phone for one month. If a relapse occurs on their phone again after the month is up, I will ask them to remove internet access until sobriety has been established for a six-month period.
- If my spouse visited a strip club, I would ask them to donate $50 to an organization that rescues individuals from the sex-trafficking industry. If my spouse visits any kind of strip club or massage parlor again, the self-imposed fine will double, then triple, and so on.

- I will ask my spouse to make an appointment with their counselor, pastor, or group leader for advice and accountability.
- I will ask my spouse to read healing-oriented literature about shame issues, boundaries, addiction, codependency, trauma, betrayal, and restoring trust.

The logical consequences for infidelity can be more serious:

- I will ask my spouse to immediately schedule a counseling appointment and disclose to me and their group leader and/or pastor.
- I will ask my spouse to arrange STD testing for me and my spouse.
- I will ask my spouse to move out of our home (or stay in another room) for a minimum of _____ months to give me time to process the affair. At the end of that time period, we will discuss the future of our marriage, which may need to be with the support of a marriage counselor. If my spouse is still involved with the individual or has not shown commitment to our marriage, I will need to seek counseling advice and initiate a separation or divorce proceedings.
- I will ask my spouse to tell our close family, friends, and pastor what has happened so I don't have to be the secret keeper or the one to take on the responsibility of letting our family know what happened.

For an exhaustive list of potential consequences, visit **puredesire.org/resources**.

BETRAYAL TRAUMA SYMPTOMS

As mentioned in Chapter Nine, here's a list of potential symptoms that might indicate this is what you're dealing with:[81]

- Intrusive thoughts and images
- Nightmares or flashbacks
- Avoidance of behaviors
- Hypervigilance
- Irritability or angry outbursts
- Insomnia
- Fearfulness
- Social withdrawal
- Feeling emotionally numb
- Physical symptoms of tension headaches, migraines, and fatigue

Some of the less tangible symptoms might include:

- Shame, guilt, and self-blame
- Depression
- Low self-esteem and self-worth
- Negative beliefs about self and others
- Unexpected mood swings
- Difficulty regulating emotions

[81] MindWell Psychology NYC, "Top Betrayal Trauma Signs, Triggers & Strategies to Recovery," October 12, 2021, **https://mindwellnyc.com/top-betrayal-trauma-signs-triggers-strategies-to-recovery-2022/**.

- Inability to trust
- Difficulty maintaining relationships or allowing others to become close to you
- Difficulty with intimacy
- Difficulty believing in your own decision making abilities

It's so important to understand and recognize when you're experiencing betrayal trauma. Often, it can be the underlying problem that rears its head in many of the symptoms listed above. But knowing this is what you're dealing with is the first step in your recovery.

THREE CIRCLES EXERCISE[82]

To some extent, healing from betrayal can feel like a matter of life or death.[83] This is especially true if your spouse doesn't pursue their own recovery or if you can't move forward in your healing. Many partners are faced with this dilemma. But, if you're willing

[82] Sex Addicts Anonymous, *Three Circles*, 1991. While this tool was originally created for recovery, over the past 30 years, it has been used in many counseling arenas to help people find healing.

[83] Heather Kolb and Ashley Jameson, *Betrayal & Beyond: Healing the Trauma of Sexual Betrayal* (Troutdale: Pure Desire Ministries International, 2022), 237-241.

to identify and walk out the plan you create through the Three Circles, you will not only survive this season of life, you will also learn to live out the healthy life God has planned for you. The Three Circles exercise can help you determine activities that proactively contribute to your healing and help you keep moving forward on your journey, regardless of the choices your spouse makes.

The **Three Circles** exercise is designed to give you a very clear and convenient method of displaying all you have discovered so far about yourself and what you need to make strides in your healing. The explanation of the circles is followed by the actual graphic of the circles. You can write your own information in the circles based on what you learn from the explanation and examples.

The **INNER CIRCLE** describes experiences, coping strategies, and situations that cause you the most harm, fear, and lack of safety. **This is the area you're trying to avoid.** This includes thoughts, feelings, and behaviors you choose to avoid because they are harmful to you. The things listed in the INNER CIRCLE can become a fiery dart or weapon the enemy can use against you.

Inside the **INNER CIRCLE** write down the thoughts, feelings, and behaviors you want to avoid. This is a one-day-at-a-time process, where God is asking you to trust Him and walk TODAY by His grace. God will provide the grace you need one day at a time, but you have to know where to apply it, thus the priority of the INNER CIRCLE.

Your **INNER CIRCLE** might include:

- Looking through my spouse's phone and/or email.
- Controlling/rescuing people or situations out of fear.

- Using anger and sarcasm to avoid addressing my true concerns and voicing my needs.
- Medicating my feelings of loneliness or worthlessness with food, alcohol, or drugs.
- Crossing my own boundaries to please someone else.
- Spending time in unhealthy places with unhealthy people.
- Allowing myself to indulge in "dark thinking" and feelings of hopelessness.
- Avoiding connection and relationship with healthy same-sex friends.

Next is the **MIDDLE CIRCLE**. These are the things that could potentially trigger you, leading you back to your INNER CIRCLE behaviors, which are harmful to you. The MIDDLE CIRCLE includes the thoughts, feelings, and behaviors that fall in the middle: between what is harmful to you and what is contributing to your healing and reflects the life God wants for you.

These **MIDDLE CIRCLE** behaviors can lead you back to the INNER CIRCLE, so developing strong boundaries and being intentional about living in health is imperative. In this circle, list thoughts, feelings, people, places, situations, and behaviors that you want to avoid because they trigger you.

Your **MIDDLE CIRCLE** might include:

- Feeling angry, isolated, or frustrated for an extended period of time.
- Allowing myself to spend time fantasizing about a better life.
- Overdoing all of it: overeating, overspending, overserving, over …

- Allowing black-and-white (all or nothing) thinking to dominate my thoughts.
- Pleasing others to feel good about myself.
- Being ticked off and cursing.
- Procrastinating on daily/routine tasks.
- Allowing perfectionism to dominate my thoughts and behaviors.
- Unable to say "no" and set healthy boundaries.

Finally, the **OUTER CIRCLE** is all about healthy behaviors that reinforce your healing. Write thoughts, feelings, behaviors, people, places, and activities that support your healing and the healthy boundaries you have in place. This might also include long-term self-care behaviors and plans to maintain connection with others.

Your **OUTER CIRCLE** might include:

- Regularly recite the specific personal promises God has given me.
- Read/listen to books on healing from betrayal, setting healthy boundaries, and other related topics.
- Spend more time having fun, whatever that looks like: alone, with my spouse, with my kids, and with same-sex friends.
- Learn to listen to myself and respect myself enough to set healthy boundaries.
- Explore new hobbies and interests in my life.
- Continue to expand my emotional awareness, identifying and expressing my feelings in a healthy way.

- Develop relationships with same-sex Christians I admire.
- Develop healthy peer friendships with same-sex friends who also desire a Christ-centered life.
- Develop a meaningful and deep devotional life.
- Focus on doing something healthy every day, not having an "all-or-nothing" mindset.
- Develop healthy eating habits and a workout schedule.
- Regularly spend time on self-care.
- Learn how to really relax when needed: spend time being still and silent.
- Use the FASTER Scale to become more self-aware and do a Double Bind when I find myself facing a challenge.
- Review my Three Circles Exercise weekly and stay in community with at least two same-sex friends.
- Review my Safety Action Plan every few months and update it accordingly.
- Commit to going through a Betrayal & Beyond group.
- Pay it forward to help others and eventually become a Betrayal & Beyond leader/co-leader.

HERE IS AN EXAMPLE OF THE THREE CIRCLES EXERCISE:[84]

Inner Circle – Behaviors and activities I want to avoid because they are harmful to me.

Example: Looking through my husband's phone to avoid being blindsided; Controlling situations and people out of fear; Using anger and sarcasm to avoid voicing my needs.

Middle Circle – Behaviors or activities to avoid because they can lead me back to my Inner Circle.

Example: Allowing myself to spend time fantasizing about a better life; Overdoing all of it: overeating, overspending, overserving, over…; Pleasing others to feel good about myself.

Outer Circle – Behaviors and activities that are healthy and support my healing.

Example: Spend more time having fun, whatever that looks like: alone, with my spouse, with my kids, with friends…; Learn to listen to myself and respect myself enough to set healthy boundaries; Explore new healthy hobbies and interests in my life.

---

[84] The Three Circles exercise used here is an adaptation of the Three Circles used by Sex Addicts Anonymous. The original is available through Sex Addicts Anonymous and pamphlets are available online through the SAA store or by telephone or postal mail from the ISO office. www.sexaa.org.

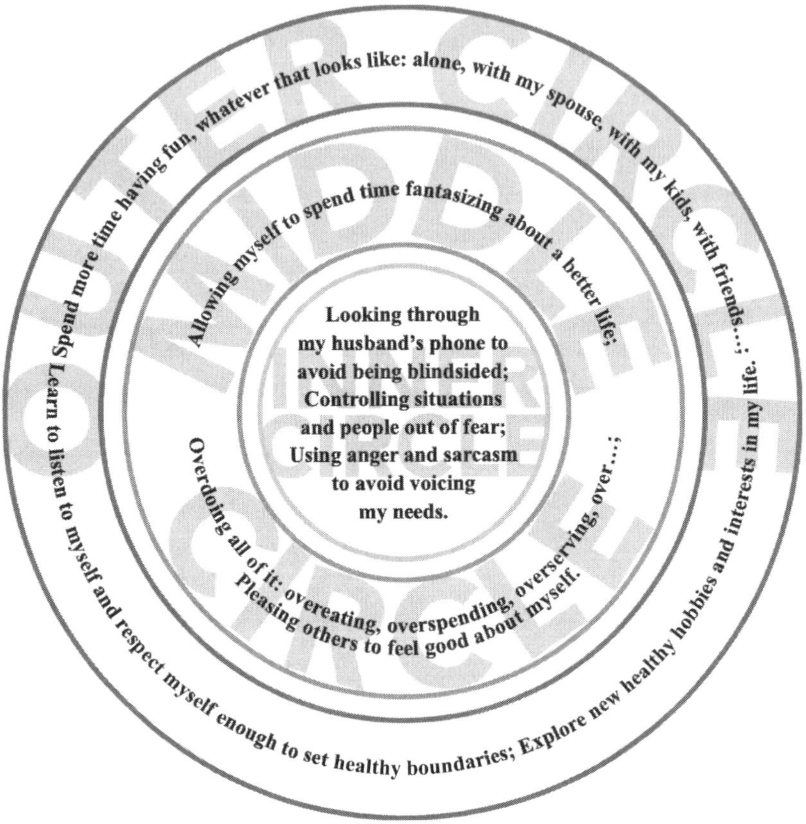

A blank Three Circles Exercise is provided. Remember, this is a document in progress. At least once every three to six months you should revisit this exercise and adjust your responses to align with your current level of healing. You will find that this is an excellent indicator of the progress you have made and an invaluable tool in recognizing the progress you've made in your healing.

MY THREE CIRCLES EXERCISE

Inner Circle – Behaviors and activities I want to avoid because they are harmful to me.

Middle Circle – Behaviors or activities to avoid because they can lead me back to my Inner Circle.

Outer Circle – Healthy behaviors and activities that are healthy and support my healing.

ABOUT THE AUTHORS

NICK STUMBO

Nick is an author, speaker, and the Executive Director for Pure Desire Ministries. He is a third generation pastor and Pastoral Sex Addiction Professional.[85] After facing his own addiction to pornography, Nick and his wife, Michelle, found hope and healing through the counseling and group ministries of Pure Desire. It radically changed their lives!

Nick has authored two books: *Setting Us Free: An Unexpected Journey of Grace* and *Safe: Creating a Culture of Grace in a Climate of Shame*. He continues to believe that the Church can become a place of healing and that Pure Desire is leading the way. Nick lives with his wife and family in the Nashville area.

FOR MORE INFORMATION ABOUT NICK AND HIS SPEAKING AVAILABILITY, visit **puredesire.org/nick**.

[85] Through the International Institute for Trauma & Addiction Professionals (IITAP).

ASHLEY JAMESON

Ashley is an author, speaker, and Director of Projects and Partnerships for Pure Desire Ministries. She is a Pastoral Sex Addiction Professional[86] and has been trained in the Multidimensional Partner Trauma Model.[87] She has overcome her own love and sex addiction and found healing from betrayal trauma through the Pure Desire group experience.

Ashley is the author of *Girl Talk: A Guide to Help Moms & Daughters have Honest Conversations about Sex* and coauthor of *Betrayal & Beyond, Unraveled: Managing Love, Sex and Relationships*, and *Authentically You*. Ashley and her husband, Jon, are working to raise their children with grace and understanding about being sexually healthy. She is passionate about helping teens, their parents, and leaders feel equipped to go against the grain and navigate the culture. Ashley lives with her husband and family in the Nashville area.

FOR MORE INFORMATION ABOUT ASHLEY AND HER SPEAKING AVAILABILITY, visit **puredesire.org/ashley**.

[86] Through the International Institute for Trauma & Addiction Professionals (IITAP).

[87] Through the Association of Partners of Sex Addicts Trauma Specialists (APSATS).